PATRIK IAN M

THE **6 PILLARS** OF

DECISION MAKING

65 TECHNIQUES &. HACKS

TO MAKE SMART AND STRATEGIC CHOICES, QUICKLY

Table of Contents

Introduction

In a world filled with countless paths and infinite possibilities, decision-making can feel like piecing together a jigsaw puzzle with an ever-changing image. As such, there are those moments of uncertainty, standing at the crossroads of choices, unsure which path will lead to fulfillment and success. Likewise, the challenge lies not only in making a decision but also in making the right one that aligns with our goals, values, and aspirations. However, identifying and understanding the common pitfalls and challenges accompanying decision-making can equip us with the tools and knowledge needed to make informed choices.

One significant challenge in decision-making today is the overwhelming volume of data and information. With numerous information sources, discerning the important from the unimportant becomes challenging. Not to mention the constant distractions that hinder our focus on the task. Yet, by embracing a structured approach to decision-making, we can effectively sift through the noise, honing in on the crucial information necessary for making well-informed choices.

Apart from aiding us in tackling modern challenges, effective decision-making also serves as a potent catalyst for personal growth and development. Making informed choices fosters confidence, cultivates new skills, and propels us toward our goals. Embracing strategic thinking and a structured approach to decision-making enables us to proactively shape our lives and manifest the future we aspire to.

The six pillars of decision-making, as outlined in this book, offer a dependable framework to ensure decisions are rooted in logic, data, and strategic thinking. You will find 65 techniques, tips, and strategies on making confident and effective decisions peppered throughout the entire book. It's intentionally designed this way to serve as your guide along each step of the process. These techniques have undergone rigorous testing and refinement by experts across various fields, demonstrating their effectiveness in diverse situations. No matter your professional status, background, or vocation, this book provides the essential tools and knowledge to empower you in making confident and effective decisions.

In this book, you can expect to learn how to:

- Define the problem, clarify goals and objectives, and identify decision criteria.

- Analyze available information, gather data, and evaluate the pros and cons of each option.

- Generate and identify viable options, and assess their merits.

- Effectively identify and manage risks, assessing and mitigating them while accounting for external factors that may impact decision-making.

- Utilize logic and judgment to make the final decision while effectively communicating your choice.

- Create an action plan, establish deadlines, and measure progress to ensure the successful implementation of your decision.

As an individual who has faced numerous decisions in both personal and professional spheres, I recognize the value of a structured decision-making approach. I have encountered the stress of making swift choices with considerable implications for my future and the apprehension of potentially erring. Nevertheless, through experience, employing a structured decision-making process equips me to make more informed and strategic choices.

By making higher-quality decisions, you enhance the likelihood of favorable outcomes. Becoming a better, more effective decision-maker begins with tackling one decision at a time. My realization of this concept led me to devise practical solutions and strategies to avoid pitfalls between my desired decisions and their execution.

Then, this fascination drove my resolve to improve as a decision-maker. The principles I uncovered became almost second nature by consistently analyzing and practicing what I learned. Now, through this book, I share my knowledge, making the information accessible to anyone interested in exploring and acquiring decision-making skills that have inspired success among individuals from all walks of life.

Hence, the ultimate aim of this book is to help you fortify your decision-making abilities, allowing you to recognize habits and behaviors that may mislead or hinder you when faced with decisions. If you seek to retrain yourself and boost your confidence in making superior decisions, this book will guide how to achieve that transformation.

Chapter 1:
Decision-Making Essentials

In the tapestry of our lives, decision-making weaves the threads that bind our experiences together. Our choices can shape our personal and professional journeys, carving paths toward success, fulfillment, and growth. By understanding the essentials of decision-making, we empower ourselves to make more informed choices that align with our values and aspirations, ultimately enriching our lives.

At its core, decision-making is the process of selecting an option from many alternatives. This chapter will illuminate the three primary components that form the foundation of every decision: *choice, information, and preference*. Together, these elements converge to create the framework within which we navigate the complexities of our lives.

As we delve deeper into this fascinating topic, we will uncover the different types of decisions that permeate our lives: *strategic, tactical, and operational*. Each uniquely shapes our experiences, guiding us toward our goals and facilitating our progress. By comprehensively exploring these decision types, we will equip ourselves with the knowledge and tools necessary to harness the power of informed decision-making.

With curiosity as our compass and enthusiasm as our guide, we will traverse this enlightening landscape, unlocking the secrets to making choices that elevate our lives to new heights.

What Is a Decision?

Likely, everyone encounters a myriad of choices and opportunities. At the core of these choices lies the concept of decision-making. A decision transcends a mere selection; it is a thoughtful process encompassing evaluating alternatives and commitment to a course of action. Grasping the essence of a decision is crucial as it equips us with the ability to make informed choices in alignment with our goals and values.

When making a decision, we face an array of alternatives. These options represent various paths, each with a unique set of potential outcomes and consequences. Decision-making necessitates active engagement as we meticulously assess these alternatives, contemplating the risks, benefits, and trade-offs involved. Thus, it is a purposeful process that calls for critical thinking to choose the option best aligned with our desired outcomes.

Examining the characteristics of a decision highlights its importance in our lives. Decisions are deliberate and purposeful, influenced by desires, goals, and aspirations. As a result, our decision-making process is directed by our intended accomplishments and the path we seek to follow in life. Nonetheless, various internal and external factors can often shape choices, including personal beliefs, values, emotions, social pressures, cultural norms, and situational contexts. In other words, our decision-making occurs within a broader framework of influences that steer our thoughts and choices. Understanding these characteristics enables us to appreciate the intricacy and depth of decision-making.

Besides, decisions differ from actions or behaviors as they involve conscious evaluation of alternatives and dedication to a specific course of action. They comprise intentional and thoughtful choices, unlike random or impulsive actions that lack careful consideration of potential outcomes. Acknowledging this distinction fosters a more strategic and mindful approach to decision-making.

Components of a Decision

The decision-making process involves a complex interplay of components that guide us in determining the best option. Three key elements form the foundation of any decision: *choice, information, and preference.*

Choice

In decision-making, a choice is selecting between two or more options. Sometimes, decisions need us to choose from many options, while others might only require us to pick between two. Regardless of the number of options, each decision involves making some trade-offs. A **trade-off** is defined as gaining or losing one thing for the benefit of another.

Having alternatives and options plays a crucial role when making a choice. **Alternatives** provide backup options if our initial choice does not work out as expected. Meanwhile, **choices** allow us to consider different routes and possibilities and make informed and well-thought-out decisions.

Several internal and external factors can influence the choices available to us. Internal factors such as *personal beliefs, values, desires, and past experiences* can impact our decision-making ability. Moreover, external factors like *social norms, cultural influences, and situational context* must also be considered.

Considering that, before making a choice, understand the array of alternatives and options at hand. This process entails gathering information, researching various possibilities, and pinpointing potential solutions to the problem or challenge. Consequently, being well-informed empowers us to make educated choices.

Upon identifying a range of alternatives and options, weigh the pros and cons of each choice. As such, examine each alternative's potential benefits and drawbacks, evaluate the associated risks, and comprehend the trade-offs accompanying each decision.

Then, the final step in making an informed choice involves contemplating each option's potential outcomes and consequences. Hence, look beyond immediate advantages or disadvantages and consider the long-term implications of our decisions on aspects such as our lives, careers, and relationships.

Information

Information plays a pivotal role in decision-making. For instance, the **right information** helps illuminate and clarify your choices. Conversely, wrong information can mislead you. Therefore, the first step in making an informed decision is gathering all relevant information.

One of the most significant challenges in gathering information is identifying reliable sources. The internet and social media have created an overwhelming amount of information. Yet, not all sources are trustworthy. Based on that, you must identify authoritative, unbiased, and reputable sources. Look to government organizations, academic institutions, well-established industry associations, or websites with a well-earned reputation for accuracy and quality of content.

After identifying reliable sources, the next step is to assess the quality and credibility of the information. To evaluate the quality and credibility of information, consider the following questions:

- *How was the information collected, and by whom?*

- *Is the information factual and accurate?*

- *Is the information presented clearly and concisely?*

- *Is the information free from bias or prejudice?*

- *Is the information relevant to the decision at hand?*

While assessing the quality and credibility of information, consider whether it is complete and relevant to the decision at hand. Incomplete information can cloud judgment and lead to poor decision-making. Additionally, irrelevant information is detrimental to the decision-making process, leading decision-makers astray and affecting their ability to make an informed decision.

To acquire and evaluate information effectively, use *data analysis, market research, competitive analysis, cost-benefit analysis, and statistical modeling.* These techniques aid in acquiring accurate and relevant information, which in turn, helps decision-makers to make informed and effective decisions.

Overall, recognize that your **decision-making process will only be successful if based on sufficient information** or with the necessary information.

Preference

Individuals have unique *emotions, values, and priorities* influencing their decision-making process. For instance, if you have a strong emotional attachment to a certain car brand, you may be more willing to overlook some of its flaws than a brand you feel no emotional connection to. **Values**, on the other hand, guide our decision-making by laying out what we perceive as necessary. **Priorities** can also impact decision-making by forcing us to choose between multiple options based on their urgency.

When making decisions, consider the alignment of choices with personal goals and values. For example, if one of your goals is to live a healthy lifestyle, you may be more inclined to choose healthy food options. If one of your values is environmental awareness, you may be more likely to select eco-friendly products. Understanding what matters to you can guide your decision-making. Likewise, it ensures that your choices align with your values and goals.

However, preferences must be balanced with rational decision-making to make a well-informed decision. **Logic and objective criteria** should be incorporated into the decision-making process. As such, keep emotions and biases aside, as they can cloud our judgment. **Weighing each decision's pros and cons** and considering each situation's outcomes will also help make an informed decision.

Interconnection Between the Components

Every choice we make is shaped by the information we possess or pursue. For instance, when searching for a new car, your considerations will be influenced by your knowledge of available vehicles. This principle also applies to other decisions, such as selecting a restaurant or vacation destination. Consequently, our preferences often dictate the type of information we seek.

Preferences also play a pivotal role in our decision-making process. When choosing between two options, we often weigh competing preferences. For example, you might opt for a faster car over an eco-friendly one if speed holds greater importance than reducing your carbon footprint. However, preferences are fluid and can change based on circumstances, environment, and experiences. As a result, today's choices may differ from those made tomorrow.

The interaction between choice, information, and preference is iterative and dynamic. We constantly evaluate our preferences and adapt to new information. Moreover, our choices influence our future preferences by affecting the information we seek, thus creating a feedback loop between choice and preference. Through continued decision-making, we learn and refine our preferences further.

Importance of Decision-Making

The significance of decision-making extends beyond individual choices and holds immense importance in various fields, including:

Business and Management

In business and management, decision-making plays a role in determining the success and competitiveness of organizations. Effective decision-making impacts factors such as organizational growth, profitability, and sustainability. It enables efficient resource allocation, ensuring that available resources are utilized optimally. Decision-making also involves assessing risks and developing mitigation strategies, fostering a risk management culture. Additionally, strategic planning and goal achievement are guided by well-informed decisions while promoting innovation and adaptability in dynamic business environments.

Healthcare

The healthcare sector heavily relies on sound decision-making to deliver quality patient care. Decision-making in healthcare involves critical aspects such as patient care and treatment planning, ensuring the best possible outcomes for individuals. It also encompasses resource allocation and budgeting, optimizing the allocation of limited resources to provide optimal healthcare services. Ethical considerations guide decision-making, upholding patient autonomy and ensuring favorable patient outcomes. Moreover, efficient decision-making enhances healthcare system efficiency, streamlining processes and improving overall patient experience.

Education

Decision-making in education impacts curriculum development, shaping the learning experiences of students. It involves choosing appropriate instructional strategies to cater to diverse learner needs. Additionally, decision-making is vital in student assessment, providing insights into academic progress and informing educational interventions. Allocation of resources and budget planning is also guided by decision-making, ensuring efficient use of educational resources. Ultimately, decision-making in education aims to promote student success and equip them for future opportunities.

Public Policy and Governance

Public policy and governance rely on effective decision-making to address societal challenges and drive development. Decisions made in public policy impact the overall progress of societies, influencing areas such as infrastructure, social welfare, and economic growth. The efficient allocation of public resources is crucial, as decision-making determines where investments benefit the community. Addressing complex social challenges requires thoughtful decision-making, considering the diverse needs and perspectives of the population. Moreover, decision-making in public policy promotes transparency and accountability, ensuring that decisions are made in the public's best interest.

Personal Life

In our personal lives, decision-making influences various aspects that shape our well-being and future. Career choices and professional development rely on informed decision-making to identify opportunities aligned with our interests and goals. Financial planning and investment decisions require careful analysis and decision-making to secure our financial future. Decision-making in health and lifestyle choices impacts our overall well-being and quality of life. Additionally, decision-making helps build relationships and foster personal growth, allowing us to make choices that nurture meaningful connections and personal development.

Hence, developing strong decision-making skills is essential for success and growth in various areas.

Different Types of Decisions

In the world of decision-making, we can make various types of decisions, each with its own unique characteristics and implications. These decisions can be broadly categorized into three types: *strategic, tactical, and operational.*

Strategic

Strategic decisions are made at high organizational levels, significantly impacting its long-term trajectory. Typically, senior leaders such as CEOs or board members are responsible for decisions that determine the organization's direction and priorities. As such, it encompasses entering new markets, acquiring competitors, or introducing new product lines. To make such decisions, a comprehensive understanding of the organization's objectives is necessary. Furthermore, a firm grasp of available resources, awareness of the competitive landscape, and readiness to take risks and pursue bold initiatives are also essential.

Tactical

Tactical decisions are made at an intermediate level within an organization, predominantly influencing its immediate operations. Managers or department heads often make these decisions, including resource allocation, project management, and process optimization. Examples of tactical decisions include modifying staffing levels, restructuring departments, or deploying new software systems. These decisions necessitate a thorough comprehension of the organization's operational aspects and the capacity to juggle competing priorities while managing trade-offs.

Operational

Finally, operational decisions are made at a lower level within an organization, directly affecting its day-to-day functioning. Front-line employees often make these decisions involving task execution, problem-solving, and workflow management. Examples of operational decisions include shift scheduling, addressing customer complaints, or fixing equipment. These decisions demand an in-depth comprehension of the organization's processes and the ability to make swift and effective decisions under pressure.

Although distinct, the three types of decisions—*strategic, tactical, and operational*—are interconnected. **Strategic decisions** establish the organization's direction and priorities. Meanwhile, **tactical decisions** facilitate the execution of that vision. Then, **operational decisions** ensure effective task completion. To make well-informed decisions, understand how these different decision types interrelate and balance short-term and long-term priorities.

Furthermore, each decision type necessitates distinct processes and tools. For instance, strategic decisions may require an extensive analysis of market trends, customer needs, and competitor strategies. In contrast, operational decisions often call for swift and decisive responses to prevent disruptions in daily operations. By recognizing the various decisions we make, we can adapt our decision-making approach accordingly, increasing effectiveness and achieving better outcomes.

Pillar 1:
Define

Under Pillar 1 are the fundamental steps of defining a decision, laying the groundwork for effective decision-making by elucidating the issue and collecting vital information. This Pillar comprises *Chapter 2: "The Wh Questions" and Chapter 3: "Documenting."*

For instance, **Chapter 2** emphasizes the importance of posing and answering critical questions to understand the decision-making process better. As such, it highlights the significance of defining goals and pinpointing factors contributing to the problem. Moreover, this chapter explores the necessity of identifying relevant individuals, seeking additional information when necessary, and contemplating the timing and location of the issue.

Advancing to **Chapter 3** lies in the importance of meticulously documenting the problem. The chapter offers guidance on effectively recording the issue using written descriptions in paragraph form. Likewise, it underscores the need for precision and thoroughness in capturing the problem's essence. Additionally, this chapter addresses the benefits of elaborating on the problem with supplementary details, which enhances the understanding of the issue and promotes more informed decision-making.

Adhering to the principles outlined in Pillar creates a strong foundation for their decision-making process. Clarifying the problem, gathering pertinent information, and comprehensively documenting it paves the way for well-informed decisions that yield successful outcomes.

Chapter 2:
The WH-Questions

Imagine you find yourself facing a critical decision, one that could have far-reaching consequences for your business. As you stand at the crossroads, uncertain about which path to take, you realize that the key to making an informed choice lies in asking the right questions. The *wh-questions* become your guiding light, illuminating the path toward clarity and understanding. *What decision needs to be made? Why is this decision necessary? What are the goals to be achieved?* By exploring these fundamental questions, you embark on a journey of exploration and discovery, peeling back the layers of complexity and gaining invaluable insights. The importance of *wh-questions* in decision-making cannot be overstated; they serve as the compass that guides you toward making well-informed choices, leading to successful outcomes.

What Decision Must You Make?

At the intersection of numerous decisions, we encounter a pivotal question that drives us forward: *What decision must be made?* This seemingly simple yet profound query holds the potential to mold our lives, reshape our paths, and actualize our dreams. Nonetheless, the answer to this question is not always immediately evident. As such, it requires introspection, examination, and a profound comprehension of our circumstances, objectives, and values.

Once you have defined the decision, delve deeper by asking the *wh-questions: who, what, when, where, why, and how.* These questions are valuable tools for a comprehensive understanding of the decision and the factors that must be considered.

By asking *"who,"* you can identify the individuals or stakeholders impacted by the decision, allowing you to consider their perspectives and potential concerns. The question of *"what"* helps you assess the potential consequences of each available option, providing insights into the risks, benefits, and outcomes associated with different choices.

Understanding *"when"* the decision needs to be made enables you to establish timelines and prioritize actions accordingly. By considering *"where"* the decision will be implemented, you can anticipate the environmental or contextual factors that may influence the outcome or execution of the decision.

Asking *"why"* provides a deeper understanding of the importance and rationale behind the decision, connecting it to your goals, values, and desired outcomes. Lastly, the question of *"how"* guides you in formulating an effective action plan and determining the necessary steps to implement the decision successfully.

By incorporating the *wh-questions* into your decision-making process, you gain a more holistic perspective, ensuring that you consider various dimensions and factors relevant to the decision. This comprehensive approach enhances the quality of your decision-making, increases the likelihood of making informed choices, and paves the way for more successful outcomes.

Considering these questions can help you gather information and evaluate the decision from different angles. Likewise, it helps identify potential obstacles you may not have considered otherwise. Thus, taking the time to ask yourself the right questions can help you better understand your decision.

Why Make This Decision?

Questioning *"Why make this decision?"* during the decision-making process is natural. This question acts as a compass, guiding us toward clarity and purpose. As such, understanding our decisions' underlying motivations and reasons is the key to unlocking personal growth, fulfillment, and realizing our aspirations. To embark on informed decision-making, the first step is to *define your goals.*

Define Your Goals

Defining the reasons behind our decisions helps us clarify our goals and objectives, which in turn helps us make better choices. To determine your goals, start by understanding what you want to achieve. *What are the outcomes you are hoping to accomplish with your decision? Are you trying to solve a problem, reach a milestone, or improve your life?* Once you know the desired outcome, you can work backward and determine the necessary steps.

For example, let us say you decide to take a new job. Before making a decision, define your goals. *Do you want to earn more money? Are you looking for a better work-life balance? Do you want to work in a different industry?* By understanding your objectives, you can evaluate if the new job aligns with your goals and is worth pursuing.

Defining your goals also helps you prioritize your decision-making criteria. You can use your objectives to weigh the pros and cons of each option. From that point, you can determine which choice aligns best with your desired outcomes. For instance, if you aim to earn more money, you might prioritize job offers with higher salaries. Likewise, defining your goals helps you align your choices with your desired outcomes. As such, when we have clear objectives in mind, it becomes easier to evaluate our options by weighing each choice's pros and cons.

Moreover, defining your goals helps you avoid decision fatigue. **Decision fatigue** occurs when we are faced with too many choices, as our brains become overwhelmed. Subsequently, under this state, our decisions are more likely to be impulsive. However, by knowing your goals, you can focus on those that align with your objectives instead of evaluating every option. Eliminating distractions and mental clutter helps you make smarter, more strategic decisions.

Once you know where you want to go, it is easier to stay on target and not get sidetracked by the little things.

What Are the Contributing Factors?

In every organization, everyone encounters various challenges. These problems can come from various sources, significantly affecting the organization's overall operation. That said, it is important to understand that identifying the root cause of the issue is the key to resolving the problem.

Lack of Information

A significant contributing factor to decision-making problems is often insufficient information. Making informed decisions becomes challenging when there is no relevant data or inadequate research. To overcome this hurdle, actively gather as much information as possible. Conduct thorough research, analyze available data, and seek insights from experts or other stakeholders to ensure that decision-making is well-informed.

Emotional Factors

Emotions frequently contribute to decision-making problems by clouding our judgment and hindering rational thinking. When overwhelmed by emotions, making logical choices becomes difficult. To address this issue, take a step back, calm ourselves, and approach the decision with a rational mindset. By consciously managing emotions, we can reduce their influence and make more objective decisions.

Bias

Biases and prejudices, whether personal, cultural, or organizational, substantially impact the decision-making process. They can steer us from factual and logical reasoning, leading to biased decisions. Recognizing and acknowledging our biases is a crucial step toward resolving this issue. By striving for objectivity and considering different perspectives, we can minimize the impact of bias on decision-making.

Time Constraints

The pressure of making decisions within limited time frames often results in rushed and inadequate choices. Important factors may be overlooked, and decisions may lack sufficient consideration or information. To tackle this challenge, prioritize the most critical factors and allocate time accordingly. Setting realistic deadlines and resisting the urge to rush decision-making is key to making well-thought-out choices.

Complexity

Certain decisions are inherently complex, involving multiple variables and stakeholders. Navigating such complexity can make it challenging to weigh all the options and make informed decisions. Breaking the decision down into smaller components and focusing on the most critical factors is crucial. Seeking input from experts or relevant stakeholders who can provide valuable insights further aids in understanding complex issues and making more informed choices.

Understanding these factors is fundamental to making intelligent and strategic decisions. By recognizing the role of information, emotions, biases, time constraints, and complexity in decision-making, you can enhance your ability to make accurate and effective choices.

Besides that, building on your existing knowledge and expertise can help you gain a more thorough understanding of the situation. It follows that any decisions you make will advance your goals and values.

Identify What You Already Know

Effective decision-making requires exploring the factors that shape our choices. To establish a solid foundation, start by identifying your existing knowledge. By harnessing this knowledge, you can unlock valuable insights and make confident, informed decisions.

Begin by **recognizing the breadth and depth of your knowledge and expertise**. Reflect on your skills, experiences, and areas of specialization. Consider what you have learned through education, professional development, and personal growth. Acknowledge the insights gained from past experiences and their relevance to the decisions you face today. Embrace and value your existing knowledge, empowering yourself to make well-grounded decisions based on a solid foundation.

Once you recognize your existing knowledge, the next step is to **build upon it**. Although you may possess a strong foundation, seeking new information and perspectives is crucial to expand your understanding. Engage in research, consult trustworthy sources, and tap into the expertise of others to deepen your knowledge of the subject at hand. Integrating fresh insights with your existing knowledge enhances your decision-making capabilities, enabling you to consider broader possibilities and make more well-informed choices.

Identifying what you already know also involves **acknowledging areas where you have limited expertise**. Embrace humility and recognize that no one possesses all the answers. Identify the boundaries of your knowledge and understand that seeking assistance or advice is not a sign of weakness but rather a commitment to making the best decisions possible. Be open to learning from others with specialized knowledge or expertise in areas you may lack proficiency. By doing so, you broaden your perspective and access a wealth of wisdom beyond your own.

Subsequently, in decision-making, knowledge pursuit should be ongoing. Even when you feel confident in your understanding, remain open-minded and adopt a continuous learning mindset. Cultivate curiosity, actively seek new ideas and perspectives, and stay attuned to developments and trends in your field. By nurturing a thirst for knowledge, you position yourself to adapt and make well-informed decisions in an ever-evolving world.

Who Are the People Involved?

At times, decisions may solely concern you and your interests. However, in some situations, other individuals are involved in various roles and capacities, contributing to the decision-making process and being affected by its outcomes. Therefore, it is necessary to know who is involved and what impact a decision will have on them.

Reach Out to Them if You Need More Details About the Problem

Before making a decision, consider the impact of your decision on those who will be affected, such as your team members or clients. To understand their perspectives, **examine their identities**, including age, gender, and race or ethnicity, to gain insights into their priorities and values. This information can guide you in making a decision that considers the interests of all parties involved, leading to a more favorable outcome for everyone.

Moreover, **approach people with an open mind** and a willingness to listen when discussing your ideas. Take the time to understand their concerns, priorities, and expertise by actively listening and asking thoughtful questions. Ensure that you convey a genuine desire for their input, valuing their perspective rather than simply seeking compliance with regulations or policies.

In situations where it may not be feasible to involve everyone in the decision-making process, **identify the key stakeholders and prioritize their input**. By focusing on those most likely to be affected by the decision, you can ensure a more effective and equitable outcome. Seek their input to gather diverse perspectives and ensure a fair representation of interests.

Consider the most appropriate method of communication when reaching out to those involved. Depending on individual preferences and availability, you may arrange a face-to-face meeting, phone conversation, or email. Additionally, consider the urgency and complexity of the decision to determine the most suitable communication approach.

Engaging those involved in the decision-making process can yield valuable insights and perspectives. Embrace an open-minded, collaborative, and empathetic approach when discussing the decision with all affected parties. By fostering a constructive dialogue and collaboration climate, you can maximize the benefits of involving others in the decision-making process.

When Is the Issue Occurring?

Timing is everything in decision-making. As such, by considering when an issue arises, you can uncover its potential causes and devise effective solutions. However, determining the occurrence of an issue is not always straightforward. To address this challenge, data visualization tools come to your aid. For instance, in a business setting, you can employ graphs or charts to track sales or customer feedback over time, unveiling peaks and dips in performance. Examining these patterns lets you discern whether the issue is a one-time or recurring incident.

Another approach to identifying the timing of an issue involves **exploring external factors**. Suppose you encounter a decline in productivity at work; it is worth considering industry changes as a potential cause. Additionally, it is vital to assess the temporal relationship between the issue and other events or factors at play. For example, if communication difficulties arise with a team member, reflecting on their challenges or heightened stress levels can illuminate their ability to communicate effectively.

Sometimes, the timing of an issue is influenced by intangible factors like cultural or societal trends. As such, suppose you are grappling with a sensitive matter related to gender or diversity. In that case, it becomes essential to consider how societal attitudes and expectations impact the situation.

In certain instances, **conducting research or gathering data** becomes necessary to determine the timing of an issue. This might involve conducting surveys or interviews to gather feedback from customers or stakeholders. Alternatively, analyzing data from multiple sources can reveal patterns and trends that contribute to the timing of the issue.

By being mindful of the conditions under which a problem arises, you can tailor your actions to address it effectively. Thus, analyzing the timing and context of an issue allows you to develop targeted solutions and identify potential causes.

Where Is the Issue Taking Place?

Consider the problem's occurrence and its associated factors when making decisions. Start by examining your environment to identify potential causes. **Assess your physical surroundings** for any elements that may contribute to the problem. For instance, if you are experiencing a lack of productivity at work, evaluate if your workspace is conducive to efficiency.

Additionally, **evaluate the location of the issue in relation to other factors**. If there is a communication breakdown with a team member, determine if the problem is within your workplace or influenced by external factors like stress or personal issues. Likewise, **consider the potential impact on other areas of your life**.

Here are other things to consider regarding the issue's location:

1. **Identify the geographical scope**. Determine the specific geographic area where the issue is occurring. This scope could be a specific region, city, neighborhood, or even a particular setting within a larger context.

2. **Assess the demographic factors**. Consider the demographic characteristics of the location, such as the population size, age groups, cultural diversity, socioeconomic status, and any relevant demographic trends. These factors can provide valuable insights into the dynamics and potential impacts of the issue.

3. **Analyze the institutional and organizational context**. Examine the institutions, organizations, or systems directly or indirectly related to the issue. For instance, it could include government bodies, educational institutions, healthcare systems,

legal frameworks, or other relevant entities. Understanding the roles and responsibilities of these institutions can help identify potential resources, support, or barriers in addressing the issue.

4. **Evaluate the historical and cultural context**. Explore the historical background and cultural influences that shape the location. As such, examine the traditions, values, customs, and historical events that may impact the issue. Historical and cultural factors can significantly influence the perspectives, attitudes, and behaviors of individuals and communities in the area.

5. **Consider the environmental context**. Take into account the physical environment surrounding the location. This includes natural resources, climate conditions, geographical features, and any ecological aspects that may contribute to or be affected by the issue. Understanding the environmental context can reveal potential risks, opportunities, or constraints related to the problem.

6. **Engage with the community**. Seek input and perspectives from individuals, groups, and stakeholders directly affected by the issue or with relevant knowledge and experience. Engaging with the community can provide valuable insights, foster collaboration, and ensure that decision-making processes consider diverse viewpoints.

Determining where the issue occurs can help you formulate a more effective strategy for dealing with it. Once you understand the source and nature of a problem, you can develop solutions to address its underlying causes. Remember that the environment in which decisions are made impacts their outcome.

Chapter 3:
Documenting

Experiencing difficulty remembering the logic behind our decisions is common for humans. Memory can be unreliable, and the intricacies of our decision-making processes tend to fade over time.

Keeping a record of the process, whether it involves personal or professional choices, serves as a valuable instrument for introspection and future reference. Various types of documentation that can assist in decision-making will also be examined, including *written notes, audio recordings, and video footage.*

Aside from that, documenting decision-making holds significant importance for several compelling reasons. First, it **ensures that your decisions are grounded in accurate information.** By conducting thorough research and analyzing a situation before making choices, memory errors can be circumvented and reliance on guesswork minimized.

Another key benefit of documenting decision-making is the **provision of a valuable reference point for future situations**. Examining past decisions and their underlying rationale allows for identifying patterns and trends in the decision-making process. This heightened awareness enables avoiding ineffective strategies and promotes learning from past mistakes.

Additionally, documentation **serves as a means for reflection and personal growth**. Allotting time for introspection on previous decisions facilitates learning from experiences and improving decision-making processes and skills.

In any stage of life, documenting decision-making acts as a driving force for personal and professional development. It guarantees that decisions are anchored in factual information, offers an invaluable reference for future situations, and paves the way for continuous self-improvement and progression.

How to Document the Problem

The preceding section highlighted the significance of documenting the decision-making process. This section will delve deeper into documenting the problem, which is a crucial component of effective decision-making.

Properly defining the problem and tracking the process employed to resolve it are vital for ensuring accurate and effective decision-making. The following tips can assist in documenting the problem:

1. **Deconstruct the problem into smaller elements to better comprehend the issue and pinpoint root causes.** Note each component and its relation to the overall problem.

2. **Employ visual aids such as diagrams, mind maps, and flowcharts to help visualize the problem and its various elements.** These tools can reveal patterns and connections that might not be immediately obvious.

3. **Establish clear goals.** Having an objective lets you focus on desired outcomes and facilitate decisions aligning with those aims.

4. **Document the thought process and decision-making steps.** Do the documentation through written notes, audio or video recordings, or structured templates. Maintaining a record of the process allows for a deeper understanding of one's decision-making style and highlights areas for growth.

5. **Regularly review and update documentation throughout the decision-making process.** This step helps detect gaps or inconsistencies in thinking and ensures decisions are based on accurate information.

An excellent way to make decisions is to write down all the facts about a problem and then compare those facts with possible solutions. Breaking down a problem using visual aids and goals to focus your thinking are good tactics. Writing down what you think and questions that will help ensure you get accurate results.

Write in Words (Paragraph Style)

Once you have analyzed and broken down the problem into its components, document it through writing. Expressing the problem in paragraph form aids in clarifying your thoughts and identifying any gaps or inconsistencies in your reasoning.

Start by **providing a detailed description of the situation**, clearly explaining the issue and the various contributing factors. Utilize descriptive language to paint a vivid picture of the problem and its consequences. Next, **delve into the root causes of the problem**, identifying the underlying issues and factors that worsen the situation. Be specific and thorough in your analysis. After identifying the root causes, **define your goals and objectives**. *What do you aim to achieve? What specific outcomes are you seeking? Ensure your goals are well-defined to align your decisions with your desired results.*

As you write, document your thinking process and the steps you take in making decisions. This practice allows for a better understanding of your decision-making style and highlights improvement areas. **Organize your thoughts using headings and subheadings** to facilitate easy review and updates throughout decision-making. Lastly, **consistently review and update your documentation** as you progress. Updating helps identify gaps or inconsistencies in your reasoning and ensures that your decisions are based on accurate information.

Here are some additional steps when writing your decision-making process:

1. **Start with a clear introduction.** Begin by outlining the context of the decision-making process and the problem you aim to address.

2. **Define your goals and objectives.** State the desired outcomes of your decision-making process, providing a clear direction for your actions.

3. **Detail the steps involved.** Describe each step in your decision-making process, ensuring the sequence is logical and easy to follow.

4. **Explain your rationale.** Explain each decision or action, allowing readers to understand your thought process.

5. **Present alternatives and their evaluation.** Discuss other options and the criteria used to evaluate them, demonstrating thorough analysis and consideration.

6. **Use evidence and examples**. Support your decisions with relevant data, research findings, or examples to strengthen your argument and credibility.

7. **Address challenges and limitations.** Recognize potential obstacles or constraints in your decision-making process and discuss how they were addressed or mitigated.

8. **Reflect on the decision-making process.** Analyze the effectiveness of your approach, identifying areas for improvement and lessons learned.

9. **Maintain a clear and professional writing style.** Ensure your language is concise, coherent, and appropriate for your audience, avoiding jargon or overly complex terminology.

10. **Conclude effectively.** Summarize the key points of your decision-making process and emphasize the importance of the decisions made in addressing the problem or achieving the desired outcome.

The act of writing a problem in paragraph form and then reviewing the documentation continuously can ensure effective and accurate decision-making.

Make It as In-Depth as Possible

When documenting, make it as in-depth as possible. Therefore, take the time to analyze and understand the problem from all angles thoroughly. Documenting your analysis comprehensively and in detail makes the bigger picture clearer.

To make your documentation as in-depth as possible, ensure to do the following:

1. **Identify all stakeholders.** Identify who is affected by the problem. Make sure to consider their perspectives and interests when analyzing the choices. This way, you can identify potential conflicts or trade-offs that must be addressed in your decision-making process.

2. **Use multiple sources of information.** Use different sources, including data, reports, and expert opinions. By doing so, you can develop a more complete and nuanced understanding of the problem. Hence, ensuring that your decisions are based on accurate and reliable information.

3. **Analyze the problem from different angles.** Consider the problem from multiple perspectives, such as financial, legal, ethical, and social. You will then get a broader view of the problem. From there, your decisions become well-rounded.

4. **Break down the problem into smaller components.** As mentioned earlier, a structured approach can help you break down the problem into smaller, manageable components. Using this method, you can identify specific areas that need to be addressed. Additionally, you will avoid overlooking any important factors.

5. **Consider alternative solutions.** After analyzing the problem in-depth, consider alternative solutions. Weigh the pros and cons of each option to reach the best course of action.

Besides that, here are some additional strategies that may be helpful:

- **Use visual aids.** Sometimes, visual aids such as diagrams, charts, and graphs can be more effective than written descriptions in conveying complex information. Consider using visual aids to illustrate key concepts or relationships within the problem and help to clarify your analysis.

- **Use scenario planning.** Scenario planning involves developing and analyzing multiple future scenarios with different assumptions and potential outcomes. Using scenario planning to analyze the problem, you can better understand the potential risks and opportunities associated with different courses of action.

- **Consider the emotional impact.** Taking into account the practical and logical aspects of the problem is essential. In addition to considering the emotional impact that it may have on stakeholders, this can help you to develop a more empathetic and nuanced understanding. Then, you can ensure that your decisions consider those affected's emotional needs and concerns.

- **Think beyond the immediate problem.** In some cases, the root cause of a problem may lie outside of the immediate situation. Consider the broader context in which the problem occurs, and explore potential connections. This step will help you develop a more holistic understanding of the problem and identify solutions that address underlying systemic issues.

- **Assess the opportunity cost.** The process involves considering what you would give up by choosing one option over another.

If you account for what is lost by taking one action rather than another, you can make more strategic decisions.

Making your documentation as in-depth as possible is crucial in the decision-making process. To make good decisions, you must analyze a problem from all angles and document your analysis thoroughly. Using the strategies discussed in this section, including visual aids and considering how various scenarios might affect people emotionally, you can make your analysis even more thorough. Investing time and energy in thorough documentation will help you make better decisions, which leads to more successful outcomes.

Be Precise

In documenting a problem, ensuring accuracy in analysis and description is crucial. As such, it involves collecting all pertinent information and data before meticulously examining it to pinpoint the primary issues and contributing factors. The following suggestions can help enhance precision when documenting a problem:

1. **Clarify key terms.** Enhancing precision involves defining crucial terms and concepts relevant to the problem, ensuring a common understanding and language among stakeholders. Take time to explain technical terms or industry jargon that may be ambiguous.

2. **Incorporate specific examples.** Utilize concrete examples to illustrate essential points and offer context when describing the problem. This approach aids stakeholders in comprehending the issue and its impact while making the analysis more persuasive.

3. **Employ quantitative data**. Use numerical data and analysis to reinforce arguments and conclusions whenever feasible. This method improves objectivity and precision, revealing trends and patterns otherwise unnoticed.

4. **Steer clear of generalizations**. Focus on particular facts and evidence while describing the problem and its causes, avoiding broad assumptions or generalizations. Be cautious not to exaggerate or overstate the issue's severity.

5. **Adopt clear and concise language.** Ensure comprehensibility by using straightforward language when documenting the problem. Refrain from overly technical or complex terminology that may confuse stakeholders. Be mindful of tone and writing style.

6. **Supply context.** Context clarifies the message's meaning. Start with an overview, explaining the message's relevance and adjusting for the target audience. Offer examples and specific details where applicable.

7. **Adapt to the audience.** Customize language, tone, and detail level based on stakeholders reviewing the analysis.

8. **Verify accuracy.** Confirm all facts, figures, and sources for accuracy and reliability, establishing credibility and preventing misunderstandings or errors.

9. **Continually refine the analysis.** Update the analysis as new information emerges, ensuring ongoing precision and relevance.

Accuracy in your documentation and analysis can build trust, credibility, and support for your decisions. With careful attention to detail and commitment to accuracy, you can create compelling documents that lead to successful outcomes. To ensure that your analysis is accurate, objective, and convincing, you can define key terms. Use specific examples; be quantitative—instead of generalizing. Then, write clearly and concisely.

Additionally, you should provide context to readers by considering their needs and experience. Likewise, double-check your analysis for accuracy before sharing it with others. Include visuals in your documentation so people can understand what is happening more easily.

A clear and precise communication style builds trust with stakeholders, creating an atmosphere of cooperation where ideas can flow freely. Being precise, then, can mitigate the risk of misunderstanding and contribute to the overall success of a decision-making process. Therefore, investing time and effort into being as precise as possible is important to increase the likelihood of achieving your desired outcomes.

Explain the Problem With Additional Details

Use the details of a problem and relevant information when explaining it to others. Then, prepare to describe the problem and your potential solutions. For instance, you may provide specific examples or outline key contributing factors.

One way to expand on a problem is using a problem tree analysis. This involves creating a visual diagram that identifies the core issue as the trunk of a tree. The contributing factors represent the smaller branches. A detailed and comprehensive understanding of the problem can be achieved by benchmarking. Moreover, identifying potential solutions or areas for further investigation can be very useful.

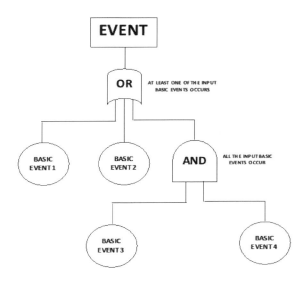

An important aspect of solving a problem is considering the potential repercussions. A sense of urgency can be created by clearly communicating the consequences. For example, if you are dealing with an issue related to defective products, it may be essential to outline the safety risks involved. In addition to providing further details and context, consider stakeholder opinions. Including various perspectives and input can help ensure that all relevant factors are considered.

Hence, a critical step in the decision-making process is to expand on a problem with additional details and information. Thoroughly documenting and analyzing a problem can improve your chances of finding solutions that work.

Add as Many Relevant Details as Possible

A well-documented decision-making process starts with understanding the significance of collecting a wide range of relevant details. Each decision encompasses unique variables, factors, and potential consequences.

Identifying and documenting these elements lays the groundwork for a thorough analysis and evaluation.

To capture relevant details effectively, **consider using a structured framework**. Begin by outlining the scope and objectives of the decision and identifying the key factors contributing to its complexity. Break down the decision into components such as goals, constraints, risks, and potential outcomes. Systematically documenting these aspects provides a comprehensive view of the decision-making landscape, enabling confident navigation through its intricacies.

Aside from that, **gather information from diverse sources**. Conduct in-depth research, consult subject matter experts, and engage with stakeholders who possess valuable insights. Each source offers a unique perspective, contributing to a more holistic understanding of the decision. Ensure the credibility and relevance of the information obtained align with the specific decision.

Incorporating quantitative and qualitative information adds depth and substance to your documentation. As such, **quantitative data** offers objective measurements and statistical evidence. Meanwhile, **qualitative information** provides subjective insights, perspectives, and experiences. Combining the two creates a well-rounded representation of the decision's context, allowing for accurate analysis and evaluation. Additionally, use visual aids such as charts, graphs, or diagrams to present complex information clearly and concisely.

Moreover, a collaborative approach can enhance the process of adding relevant details. **Engage with others** who have expertise or experience related to the decision, seek diverse perspectives, encourage open discussions, and actively listen to different viewpoints. Collaboration enriches the information pool while fostering collective ownership and commitment to the decision-making process. Emphasize effective communication and documentation of insights gained through collaboration, ensuring no valuable detail is overlooked.

Overall, effective decision-making hinges on thoroughly comprehending the problem, which is a foundation for clear and knowledgeable choices. By precisely defining the decision, we can concentrate on finding the optimal solution. This process is guided by establishing essential objectives that drive our purpose and steer decision-making. As we recognize the contributing elements of the issue, we gain valuable insights and utilize existing knowledge. Moreover, involving pertinent individuals and considering the context of the problem fosters a richer understanding and promotes collaboration. To further support this process, meticulous documentation of the issue, complete with accuracy and comprehensive details, acts as a point of reference for the analysis. Lastly, enhancing our grasp of the problem through regular supplementation with relevant information empowers us to make well-informed decisions.

Pillar 2:
Research

Gathering relevant data is essential for effective decision-making. **Chapter 4 of this pillar explores gathering relevant data** to inform your decisions. Considering both qualitative and quantitative data is essential for comprehensive insights. By recognizing the importance of both types, you ensure a deeper understanding of the factors influencing your decisions.

During the assessment phase, explore internal and external sources of data. Self-assessment also helps understand your values and biases, fostering self-awareness. External resources like books, articles, and expert opinions offer diverse viewpoints. Meanwhile, engaging with others provides new insights. Then, gathering data from various sources ensures well-informed decision-making.

Meanwhile, **Chapter 5 deals with the cognitive biases** affecting judgment and decision quality. This chapter explores the causes, signs, and impact of cognitive bias. Understanding and identifying biases are essential for objective decision-making.

Unraveling cognitive bias reveals its underlying causes, such as mental shortcuts, emotions, and social pressures. Familiarity with signs helps recognize distorted thinking. The chapter also outlines common biases, including confirmation bias, anchoring effect, groupthink, halo effect, attention bias, functional fixedness, and the Dunning-Kruger effect. Each bias influences decision-making differently. Lastly, strategies to overcome biases are also provided.

Embracing a comprehensive approach to data collection and understanding biases enhances decision-making capabilities, leading to more informed choices.

Chapter 4:
Gather Relevant Data

Data guides us through complexities and uncertainties, offering essential information for informed choices. For instance, it brings clarity in its various forms, shedding light on the path forward amid countless possibilities.

As the lifeblood of effective decision-making, data forms the factual basis upon which decisions are built, transcending speculation and intuition. Harnessing relevant data grants us a comprehensive understanding of influential factors, potential outcomes, and associated risks. Hence, it empowers us to make evidence-based, calculated decisions rather than relying on conjecture.

Subsequently, discerning and collecting the right data demands a keen eye and a strategic approach amidst the vast sea of information. This section will equip you to pinpoint vital data points, ensuring reliance on reliable and relevant information. Likewise, you will learn the common pitfalls in data collection and how to avoid them.

Type of Data

Two main types of data can be collected and analyzed: *qualitative and quantitative data.*

Qualitative Data

According to researcher Dr. Carol Grbich, *"Qualitative research is concerned with understanding people's experiences, behavior, attitudes, and perceptions from their perspective."* This data is valuable for understanding the human element of a problem. It can provide rich insights that are not measurable through numbers alone.

Qualitative data can be collected through interviews, focus groups, and observation. Collecting and analyzing this data will allow decision-makers to understand better the problem and its impact on individuals and communities.

Quantitative Data

In contrast, quantitative data focuses on measuring and analyzing numerical information. This form of data proves valuable in identifying patterns and relationships and facilitating predictions. As noted by economist Hal Varian, *"Possessing the ability to comprehend, process, extract value from, visualize, and communicate data will be an essential skill in the coming decades."* Quantitative data can be derived from various sources such as surveys, experiments, and other structured data collection methods.

Importance of Both

Qualitative data, known for its richness and depth, offers a deeper understanding of the intricacies and complexities associated with decision-making. By capturing subjective aspects such as emotions, opinions, and experiences, qualitative data uncovers human factors influencing decision-making beyond what quantitative data can reveal. Gaining insights through narratives, interviews, observations, and open-ended responses allows us to consider various perspectives and valuable context, painting a vivid picture of the situation and enhancing our ability to make informed choices.

In contrast, **quantitative data** contributes precision and objectivity to the decision-making process. Utilizing numbers, measurements, and statistical analysis, this form of data provides tangible evidence and discernible patterns. Quantitative data reveals trends, correlations, and cause-and-effect relationships, enabling us to understand a decision's scope, scale, and impact. With concrete metrics that can be compared, analyzed, and quantified, assessing different options and their potential outcomes becomes more manageable. Relying on quantitative data allows for data-driven decisions based on facts and empirical evidence, minimizing subjectivity and bias.

The true strength of qualitative and quantitative data emerges from their combined use. Together, they present a comprehensive and holistic view of the decision-making landscape. While qualitative data adds depth, context, and human insights, quantitative data supplies structure, objectivity, and measurable outcomes. Integrating these two types of data bridges the gap between comprehending intricate details and grasping broader patterns and trends. This fusion empowers us to make robust, well-rounded decisions considering human aspects and measurable impact.

Assessment

Assessing data can be likened to scrutinizing puzzle pieces before assembling them to create a coherent picture. Just as a defective puzzle piece can distort the overall image, flawed data can result in erroneous decisions. Careful assessment of gathered data guarantees that our decisions rest on a solid foundation.

Understanding the source of information is a key aspect of data assessment. Sources vary in credibility, expertise, and potential biases, making critically evaluating them essential. By doing so, we can determine the reliability and objectivity of the data, empowering us to make informed choices.

Another critical component of data assessment is the quality and completeness of the data itself. As such, ensure that data points are accurate, current, and pertinent to the decision. Examining data consistency, precision, and alignment with decision-making requirements helps assess data quality. Additionally, recognizing gaps or missing information is imperative for basing decisions on a comprehensive understanding of the situation.

The context in which data is collected significantly influences its assessment. Factors such as timing, circumstances, and underlying conditions affect the relevance and applicability of the data. Grasping the context allows for accurate data interpretation and adjustments for potential biases or limitations.

Furthermore, data assessment entails considering its compatibility with other available information. Cross-referencing data from multiple sources and perspectives validate findings, identifies patterns, and provides a more holistic view of the situation. This triangulation process bolsters data reliability and robustness, reinforcing confidence in decision-making.

In conclusion, data assessment is critical in the decision-making process for making informed choices. By evaluating the data's source, quality, context, and compatibility, we can ensure its reliability and relevance.

Internal Self-Assessment

Internal assessments serve as a window into one's skills and abilities. By dedicating time to reflect on personal strengths and weaknesses, a deeper understanding of capabilities and areas needing improvement is achieved. This process resembles closely examining a painting, where scrutinizing the details enhances appreciation for the beauty and complexity of the entire piece.

Self-assessment is a method for conducting internal evaluations. It involves taking a personal inventory of skills, interests, and experiences, which can be accomplished through journaling or completing self-evaluation forms. This snapshot of oneself at a specific moment allows for tracking progress and observing growth and change over time.

Likewise, internal assessments encompass formal evaluations, such as skills assessments or performance appraisals. These assessments assist in pinpointing areas that may require additional training or development. Like using a magnifying glass to examine skills and abilities, this approach enables a closer look at details and facilitates necessary adjustments.

Through introspection, a clearer comprehension of personal strengths and weaknesses is gained. Decision-making becomes more manageable when considering all possibilities and ruling out those deemed unsuitable. Refining a well-tuned instrument and honing skills and abilities over time cultivate more effective and confident decision-makers.

External Assessment

Recognizing that decisions are not made in isolation is essential, as they are influenced by numerous external factors shaping our operational context. External assessment serves as a tool for capturing this broader view through systematic information gathering and analysis from external sources, providing a comprehensive understanding of factors impacting our decision-making environment.

The ever-evolving business landscape, driven by technological advancements, shifting consumer preferences, and global economic trends, necessitates conducting external assessments. By gaining insight into these dynamic forces, we can identify emerging opportunities and potential threats. Thus, allowing us to navigate change with agility and adaptability, ensuring alignment with external realities.

Understanding market trends and competitor dynamics is crucial for competitive and sustainable decisions. External assessment enables market landscape analysis, trend identification, and future development prediction. Understanding competitors' strategies, strengths, and weaknesses empowers strategic positioning and competitive edge development. Leveraging this knowledge allows capitalization on market opportunities and risk mitigation.

Considering the ripple effects of decisions on society and stakeholders, external assessment incorporates societal factors such as cultural norms, social values, and ethical considerations. Understanding the broader impact of decisions ensures alignment with societal expectations and positive contributions to communities. This holistic perspective supports ethically responsible decision-making that resonates with stakeholders and promotes long-term sustainability.

External assessment involves collecting information from diverse sources, including market research reports, industry analyses, customer feedback, and expert opinions. This process requires skill in information synthesis, transforming vast amounts of data into meaningful insights for informed, evidence-based decision-making.

Pitfalls of Data Collection

Incorrect data will make your decision-making ill-informed. As such, there are four pitfalls to be avoided when dealing with data collection.

Using Poor or Incorrect Methodology

Flawed methodologies can result in unreliable data, distorted analysis, and misguided decisions. Consequently, the methodology used in data collection impacts the data's reliability and validity. **Poor methodology** encompasses flawed or inadequate techniques during the data collection process, such as biased sampling methods, poorly designed surveys or questionnaires, or inconsistent data collection procedures. Utilizing these flawed methodologies may produce skewed or unreliable data, compromising the decision-making process's integrity.

Meanwhile, the **incorrect methodology** involves using methods unsuitable for the specific data collected, like applying quantitative analysis to qualitative data or vice versa, disregarding ethical considerations, or failing to account for confounding variables. These methodological missteps can lead to erroneous conclusions and misguided decisions.

Using poor or incorrect methodology in data collection carries significant implications. Decision-makers may base their choices on inaccurate or incomplete information, leading to suboptimal outcomes. Inaccurate data can result in flawed analysis, trend misinterpretation, and poor decision-making.

Prioritizing robust and well-designed data collection methods is essential to circumvent the pitfalls of poor or incorrect methodologies. This priority includes *employing appropriate sampling techniques, ensuring clear and unbiased survey or questionnaire design, and implementing standardized data collection protocols.* Adhering to best practices in data collection enables decision-makers to enhance the reliability and validity of the information they rely on.

Lastly, comprehending the limitations of various data collection methodologies is crucial. Recognizing the strengths and weaknesses of quantitative and qualitative approaches and the importance of ethical considerations can guide decision-makers toward the most suitable methodology for their specific needs.

Not Sifting Through the Data Before Analysis

Data collection often involves amassing extensive information from various sources, such as surveys, interviews, market research, or internal systems. However, decision-makers risk basing their analysis on incomplete or irrelevant information without efficiently sifting through this data. This situation resembles attempting to solve a puzzle without organizing the pieces first; the bigger picture remains hidden.

Reviewing, organizing, and validating collected information is crucial to sifting through data before analysis. This process enables decision-makers to detect patterns, trends, and essential insights that might remain undiscovered otherwise. Employing a structured approach, like data cleaning and preprocessing techniques, allows for focusing on the truly significant data points while filtering out noise.

Furthermore, sifting through data helps uncover potential biases or errors in the collected information. It aids in identifying outliers, inconsistencies, or missing data that could impact the analysis's accuracy and reliability. Addressing these issues early ensures conclusions are based on quality data, providing a solid foundation.

Dedicating time and effort to sift through data before analysis gives decision-makers a deeper understanding of the information. As a result, they can make more accurate interpretations, draw meaningful conclusions, and ultimately make better-informed decisions. This approach fosters a data-driven mindset, where decisions are grounded in evidence rather than assumptions or intuition.

Failing to Review the Analysis

In decision-making, a critical mistake individuals often make is neglecting to review the analysis they have conducted. After investing time and effort in gathering information, analyzing data, and evaluating options, thoroughly reviewing the analysis before making a final decision is essential.

Multiple purposes are served by reviewing the analysis. First, it **enables validation of the accuracy and reliability of the gathered information**. Carefully examining the data, sources, and methodologies ensures that the analysis is based on sound and credible foundations. This validation process instills confidence in the analysis-derived conclusions, strengthening decision integrity.

Additionally, reviewing the analysis **offers an opportunity to identify potential biases or gaps in the evaluation.** It enables challenging assumptions, considering alternative perspectives, and detecting overlooked factors influencing the decision. Engaging in this review enhances the analysis's robustness and comprehensiveness, making it more reliable and insightful.

Reviewing the analysis also **allows for seeking feedback and input from relevant stakeholders or subject matter experts**. Sharing the analysis with others and inviting their perspectives can introduce fresh insights and highlight overlooked aspects. This collaborative approach promotes a more holistic decision-making process, leveraging diverse expertise and avoiding potential pitfalls.

Furthermore, reviewing the analysis **helps assess the alignment between identified options and goals, values, and priorities.** Evaluating how each option contributes to desired outcomes and determining whether adjustments or trade-offs are necessary is possible through this review. Ensuring the decision remains consistent with overarching objectives increases the likelihood of achieving desired results.

Relying Too Much on Existing Data

When relying too heavily on existing data, there is a risk of overlooking critical nuances and dynamic factors that may influence decisions. Data inherently represents past events or circumstances and may not sufficiently capture present complexities or future possibilities. It is essential to remember that decision-making often involves navigating uncharted territories and venturing into the unknown, where historical data might not provide adequate guidance.

Existing data may also be subject to inherent biases or limitations. Data collection processes, measurement methods, and sample sizes can introduce biases that skew findings. Furthermore, data might reflect only a narrow perspective or fail to capture a situation's full context. Unthinkingly relying on such data can result in misguided conclusions and ill-informed choices.

To avoid over-reliance on existing data, adopting a balanced approach that incorporates both quantitative and qualitative factors is necessary. Although data offers valuable insights, supplementing it with other information sources, such as personal experiences, expert opinions, and intuitive judgments, is crucial. This multifaceted approach allows consideration of diverse perspectives and factors not captured by existing data alone.

Lastly, embracing uncertainty and acknowledging existing data's limitations is vital. Instead of treating data as an ultimate answer, view it as one piece of the puzzle, complemented by critical thinking and analytical skills. Recognizing gaps in existing data enables exploring alternative methods, further research, or new data sources, ensuring a more comprehensive understanding of the situation.

Hence, both qualitative and quantitative data must be reliable and accurate. As such, make a conscious effort to maintain objectivity and prevent bias from influencing the process.

Chapter 5:
Check for Cognitive Bias

Flawed decisions are a common experience for all of us, often traced back to cognitive biases. These biases represent mental shortcuts our brains take when processing information, which can lead to decisions based on faulty reasoning or incomplete data.

In decision-making, it is easy to be misled by the human mind's subtle workings. Our brains are hard-wired to take shortcuts and make snap judgments, sometimes without our awareness. When not cautious, these unconscious biases can derail the decision-making process, leading to misguided choices.

Recognizing mental shortcuts and consciously working to counteract them is essential to ensure objective and well-founded decisions. Developing a keen awareness of cognitive biases, such as confirmation bias or hindsight bias, is crucial for making strategic and wise choices grounded in logic and objective analysis.

This chapter delves into various cognitive biases that can impact decision-making and offers strategies for identifying and checking for these biases. Increasing awareness of personal biases reduces the likelihood of subjective influences leading to poor decisions.

What Is Cognitive Bias?

The human mind is a complex and intricate machine involved in decision-making. Like any machine, it is susceptible to glitches and hiccups, with cognitive bias being one of the most common and insidious issues.

A cognitive bias refers to how our thinking can become skewed or distorted due to mental shortcuts based on previous experiences. These shortcuts can mislead us when making decisions. As such, cognitive bias stems from how our brains are wired. As we continuously take in vast amounts of information from our surroundings, our brains develop patterns and filters to make sense of everything. However, these patterns and filters may become too rigid, causing us to perceive the world distorted or incompletely.

Unawareness of cognitive biases can lead to serious consequences in decision-making, as we risk making poor choices based on flawed reasoning or incomplete information. We might ignore crucial facts or data points that do not align with our preexisting beliefs or overestimate our ability to predict the future based on past experiences.

Being aware of cognitive biases is essential to make smart and strategic choices. Counteracting these biases requires vigilance and ensuring that decisions are grounded in sound reasoning and objective analysis.

Causes

A variety of factors can cause cognitive biases. These may include our past experiences, upbringing, and cultural and societal influences. Such factors can all contribute to how we perceive information and make decisions. In so doing, they can create blind spots in our thinking that we may not even be aware of. Additionally, the fast-paced and complex nature of modern society can also contribute to cognitive biases. Often, we may feel pressured to make quick decisions without fully considering all the available information.

Signs

Recognizing cognitive biases can be difficult, as they often occur unconsciously and can be difficult to identify. However, some common signs of cognitive bias include favoring information that supports our preexisting beliefs. Furthermore, we may ignore facts that contradict our beliefs. When this happens, we make decisions based on emotions rather than logic. Also, cognitive biases can sometimes manifest in the form of overconfidence in our abilities. Otherwise, in a reluctance to change our minds even when presented with the knowledge that we previously did not have.

Impact

Cognitive bias has a sneaky way of infiltrating our decision-making processes, and the impact can be profound. It can cause us to cling to preconceived notions and dismiss evidence that challenges our assumptions. This can create blind spots that cloud our vision and limit our ability to see the bigger picture. In the worst cases, cognitive biases can lead to missed opportunities and poor decision-making, with long-lasting effects on our personal and professional lives.

Not only does cognitive bias impact our decision-making, but it can also strain relationships and team dynamics. When we become entrenched in our biases, we may become dismissive or defensive. We can make better decisions and build stronger relationships if we recognize the existence of cognitive biases. From that juncture, we can actively work to mitigate their effects and not let them cloud our judgment.

Common Types of Cognitive Bias

Cognitive bias can manifest itself in many ways, and several types can impact decision-making. Understanding these common types of cognitive bias is crucial to identifying and mitigating their influence on our choices. In this section, we will explore some of the most prevalent types of cognitive bias and how they can affect our decision-making processes.

Confirmation Bias

Confirmation bias, a subtle cognitive bias, can significantly impact our decision-making. It occurs when we actively search for information that supports our preexisting beliefs while ignoring or downplaying contradictory information. This behavior creates a self-reinforcing loop, making us increasingly convinced of our initial position and less willing to consider alternative viewpoints.

The insidious nature of this bias lies in the difficulty of recognizing it while experiencing it. We might genuinely believe we are objective and rational, even as we unconsciously filter out information. Overcoming confirmation bias necessitates a willingness to step outside our comfort zone, explore alternative viewpoints, and genuinely evaluate the evidence presented.

Anchoring Effect

The anchoring effect is a cognitive bias in which people rely heavily on the initial information they receive (the "anchor") when making decisions. This anchor influences subsequent judgments and shapes how individuals perceive and interpret new information.

For instance, if a salesperson begins negotiations with a high price, buyers may view all following lower prices as reasonable, even if they remain relatively high. This effect can result in irrational decision-making and hinder individuals from considering other options that could be more logical or beneficial.

To circumvent the anchoring effect, it is crucial to recognize the initial anchor and gather additional information before deciding. Doing so can avoid impulsive actions based solely on the first piece of information encountered.

Groupthink

Groupthink is a cognitive bias that arises when a group makes decisions without thoroughly considering all available options, often leading to suboptimal or flawed outcomes. This mental trap occurs when people prioritize group harmony and consensus over independent thinking and constructive debate. In such a scenario, individuals may experience pressure to conform to the dominant opinion, resulting in a lack of critical thinking, consideration of alternative perspectives, and exploration of new ideas. Consequently, the group's decision-making process becomes distorted, leading to poor decisions with long-lasting effects. Recognizing the signs of groupthink and taking steps to mitigate it are essential for making better, more informed decisions.

Halo Effect

The halo effect is a cognitive bias that arises when a person's positive impression of someone in one area influences their perception in other areas, regardless of whether it is deserved. This bias is akin to placing a "halo" over someone's head based on a positive trait. In situations where important decisions are made, the halo effect can be dangerous, causing people to overlook or downplay negative traits or actions of a person, company, or product. Besides that, the halo effect can lead to poor judgment, as individuals may assume that someone who excels in one area must be equally competent in all others.

To circumvent the halo effect, do the following:

- Adopt a critical approach to decision-making by separating overall impressions from specific attributes.

- Pursue diverse perspectives and contradictory evidence to question initial impressions.

- Focus on factual evidence and objective data rather than subjective opinions.

- Cultivate self-awareness by acknowledging biases and consistently reflecting on decision-making processes.

- Encourage open dialogue and constructive feedback to confront biases and stimulate critical thinking.

Implementing these strategies facilitates more objective and comprehensive decision-making.

Attention Bias

Attention bias involves focusing on specific information while disregarding equally or more important information. This bias can stem from various factors, such as personal beliefs, past experiences, or emotional states. For example, an individual with a negative attitude toward a certain brand may concentrate on negative news related to that brand and ignore positive news. Similarly, someone anxious about their health may fixate on symptoms they experience while neglecting other contributing factors. Aside from that, attention bias can significantly affect decision-making, leading individuals to overlook pertinent information and consequently make suboptimal choices.

In counteracting attention bias, cultivating awareness and expanding our attention is crucial. Proactively seeking varied sources of information and perspectives enables us to overcome the inclination to confirm pre-existing beliefs. A deliberate and systematic approach to gathering information, rather than relying on easily accessible data, ensures a more comprehensive evaluation. Mindfulness practices help us identify when attention bias occurs and shift our focus to alternative viewpoints. Soliciting input from others and engaging in open dialogue challenge our biases, resulting in more well-rounded decisions. By actively broadening our attention, collecting thorough information, practicing mindfulness, and embracing diverse perspectives, we can reduce the impact of attention bias and make more informed and unbiased decisions.

Functional Fixedness

Functional fixedness is a cognitive bias that restricts an individual's ability to envision an object's potential uses beyond its typical function. This tendency involves perceiving an object solely in terms of its most common or familiar use, hindering the consideration of alternative or unconventional applications. This bias obstructs problem-solving and innovation by limiting creativity and inhibiting out-of-the-box thinking.

Research has demonstrated that individuals more prone to functional fixedness are less likely to solve problems creatively. For example, a person might struggle to perceive a paperclip as anything other than a device for holding paper together, even though it could be a makeshift lock pick. Acknowledging functional fixedness allows us to overcome this inclination to view things singularly.

Likewise, there are ways to combat functional fixedness. As such, **cognitive flexibility** helps by approaching problems from different perspectives and considering unconventional uses. Meanwhile, **brainstorming** generates diverse ideas, bypassing preconceptions and fostering innovation. **Seeking inspiration** from various sources also broadens our thinking and exposes us to new approaches. Overcoming functional fixedness enhances decision-making, unleashing innovative solutions and empowering us to navigate challenges confidently.

Dunning-Kruger Effect

The Dunning-Kruger effect is a cognitive bias that influences people's ability to accurately evaluate their skills and knowledge. Individuals affected by this bias often overestimate their capabilities while underestimating the skills and abilities of others. This bias can lead to serious consequences, particularly in professional environments, where it may result in poor decision-making, subpar performance, and potential harm to others.

A deficiency in metacognition, or the capacity to reflect on one's thinking, lies at the core of the Dunning-Kruger effect. Those unskilled in metacognition might be unable to recognize their limitations, making them susceptible to this bias. To counteract the Dunning-Kruger effect, practicing self-awareness and continually critiquing one's knowledge and skills honestly is necessary.

Psychologist David Dunning emphasized that *"the road to self-insight runs through other people,"* suggesting that seeking feedback and constructive criticism from others can help mitigate the Dunning-Kruger effect. By embracing humility and a willingness to learn, we can avoid overestimating our abilities based on others' perceptions.

How to Overcome Cognitive Bias

Decision-making presents the intriguing challenge of cognitive bias. These ingrained thought patterns subtly affect our judgments and distort our perception of reality, stemming from innate cognitive processes. They impact how we interpret information, evaluate risks, and make decisions. Overcoming cognitive bias is a vital skill for enhancing rational and objective decision-making. By recognizing and addressing biases, we can attain greater clarity and accuracy in our decision-making process.

Navigating cognitive bias begins with **cultivating self-awareness**. Familiarizing ourselves with common biases like confirmation, availability, and anchoring biases enables us to identify them in action. Acknowledging predispositions and understanding their potential effects allows us to challenge and mitigate their influence.

Additionally, **seeking diverse perspectives** is necessary. Engaging with individuals of varying backgrounds, experiences, and viewpoints offers invaluable insights. Thoughtful discussions and active listening to alternative opinions counteract our natural inclination towards information that confirms preexisting beliefs. Embracing diversity broadens our perspective and enhances well-rounded decision-making.

Likewise, **employing critical thinking** helps overcome cognitive bias. This process involves objectively examining evidence, questioning assumptions, and evaluating arguments based on logic and reason. Actively scrutinizing information uncovers hidden biases and faulty reasoning, enabling more informed and unbiased decisions.

Furthermore, **using decision-making frameworks** helps reduce cognitive bias impact. Techniques like the *Deliberate Decision-Making Process or the Six Thinking Hats Method* encourage analytical thinking and diminish bias influence. These frameworks offer systematic approaches to problem-solving, gathering information, considering multiple perspectives, and weighing pros and cons, ultimately leading to balanced and rational decisions.

Lastly, **continuous learning and improvement** are essential for combating cognitive bias. Remaining curious, acquiring new knowledge, and challenging assumptions refine decision-making skills. Activities promoting cognitive flexibility, such as learning new skills or experiencing diverse situations, help break free from entrenched biases and reveal new growth opportunities.

Overcoming cognitive bias is an ongoing journey requiring dedication and self-reflection. Cultivating self-awareness, embracing diverse perspectives, applying critical thinking, utilizing decision-making frameworks, and committing to lifelong learning gradually untangle the complex biases clouding our judgment. This empowers us to make more rational, objective, and effective decisions, unlocking our full decision-making potential.

Pillar 3:
Identify

This pillar encompasses three chapters that provide invaluable insights and practical tools for navigating the intricacies of decision-making.

For instance, **Chapter 6** investigates the importance of alternatives in the decision-making process. Alternatives represent potential solutions or courses of action addressing specific problems or situations. As such, this chapter outlines a good alternative's characteristics, guiding you toward selecting the most appropriate option. These traits include being value-focused, technically sound, consistently clearly defined, comprehensive and mutually exclusive, capable of revealing fundamental tradeoffs, and collaboratively developed with those affected.

Chapter 7 accentuates the necessity of scrutinizing options from multiple perspectives. By expanding our viewpoint, we expose ourselves to a broader array of insights and possibilities. Throughout this chapter, we introduce various tools and techniques to aid you in this pursuit. These tools encompass brainstorming, engaging in meaningful conversations, utilizing wish lists, and employing creative methods. Moreover, under this chapter are factors to consider when evaluating options, such as associated costs, risks, tradeoffs, benefits, probability of success, and impact.

Mastering the concepts and techniques presented in these chapters will enhance your ability to identify and assess various alternatives. This expanded perspective empowers you to make informed decisions aligned with your goals and aspirations.

Chapter 6:
Consider Alternatives

Confronted with a problem or decision, we may instinctively gravitate toward the initial solution that emerges. Nevertheless, dedicating time to exploring numerous alternative solutions frequently results in improved outcomes. This chapter delves into the significance of contemplating various solution alternatives and the process of pinpointing them. By broadening your perspective and evaluating a diverse range of potential solutions, you enhance the likelihood of discovering an effective resolution.

What Is an Alternative?

Imagine being assigned a complex problem-solving task. After investing hours in research and data collection, you thoroughly analyze the situation from every perspective. However, uncertainty looms regarding the optimal solution. This is where the concept of alternatives emerges. An **alternative**, essentially an option or choice, serves as a potential solution to a problem, offering a range of possible answers to the question, *"What could we do to address this issue?"*

An alternative can also deviate from the initial or most common choice. It represents a divergent path, distinct route, or novel direction available for consideration. Alternative solutions prove indispensable in problem-solving, as they present varying approaches, methods, and perspectives to evaluate. Creatively exploring options unveils insights and solutions that may have been overlooked. This process paves the way for innovative breakthroughs, fresh perspectives, and comprehensive resolutions to intricate problems. To arrive at well-informed decisions, it is imperative to contemplate multiple alternatives and assess them based on their potential outcomes and consequences.

Traits of a Good Alternative

Selecting the optimal solution to a problem necessitates evaluating all potential alternatives. However, not all alternatives carry equal merit—some may be impractical or ineffective, while others offer greater promise. Therefore, it is essential to recognize the traits of a good alternative.

Feasibility is a critical factor, ensuring that the alternative is realistically achievable given the available resources and capabilities. A good alternative should also be practical and straightforward, facilitating smooth implementation.

Innovative alternative options are also valuable, as they present fresh and unique perspectives that distinguish them from other choices. Encouraging out-of-the-box thinking can lead to more creative solutions.

Adaptability is another crucial trait, enabling flexibility in accommodating unexpected challenges that may emerge. A good alternative should be versatile enough to adjust to variations and changes.

Additionally, **ethics and morality** should underpin our alternatives. Aligning with the decision-makers values and beliefs prevents conflicts and promotes harmony.

By considering these traits when assessing alternative solutions, you can identify the best action and achieve more successful outcomes. With a clear understanding of what constitutes an alternative, we can now delve into the characteristics of a good alternative.

Value-Focused

The value-focused alternative highlights the importance of considering the long-term consequences of our decisions and aligning them with our core values. By reflecting on our beliefs, principles, and aspirations, this approach enables us to make choices that lead to fulfillment and purpose.

To effectively implement the value-focused alternative, clarify and prioritize your values through introspection and thoughtful analysis of what truly matters to you personally and professionally. This process helps you understand your motivations and make decisions that resonate with your authentic self.

With our values identified, the value-focused alternative emphasizes evaluating options based on their compatibility with these core principles. It urges us to assess how each choice contributes to our value system, allowing us to make decisions that promote personal growth and satisfaction. This trait positions decision-making as an opportunity to live harmoniously with our values, fostering authenticity and personal satisfaction. As such, it empowers us to make choices driven by our internal compass rather than external factors or societal expectations.

Adopting the value-focused alternative in our decision-making process demands practice and reflection, urging us to be intentional, thoughtful, and mindful of our guiding values.

Technically Sound

In the decision-making process, assessing alternatives for technical soundness is crucial. A strong alternative should possess technical expertise, reliability, and accuracy, ensuring it aligns with industry standards, best practices, and relevant regulations, thus creating a robust framework for success.

Alternatives with technical soundness possess the knowledge and skills to address problems or achieve desired objectives effectively. By leveraging expertise and specialized techniques, these options facilitate efficient implementation while reducing the risk of potential complications. Considering technical soundness lets us trust that our choice is based on reliable principles and information.

Moreover, technically sound alternatives rely on comprehensive research and analysis. This involves gathering and evaluating data, conducting feasibility studies, and examining the practical implications of each option. Adopting a meticulous approach to information gathering guarantees that the selected alternative is well-informed and supported by solid evidence.

Alongside technical expertise and thorough research, a technically sound alternative must demonstrate high accuracy. This includes precise calculations, detailed measurements, and dependable data sources, which validate its feasibility and anticipated outcomes. Ensuring accuracy in an alternative confirms its practical viability in real-world situations.

By emphasizing technical soundness when evaluating alternatives, decision-makers can reduce risks, increase the chances of success, and instill confidence in the chosen course of action. This focus establishes a solid foundation for implementing the decision and enhances the overall effectiveness of the selected alternative.

Defined Consistently and Clearly

A comprehensive understanding of an alternative's potential advantages and disadvantages relies on defining it consistently and clearly. As such, a clear definition allows us to assess the alternative's feasibility, relevance, and potential impact on the desired outcome, preventing confusion and ineffective decision-making that can result from vague and misinterpreted alternatives.

Likewise, a clear and consistent definition of alternatives promotes effective communication and collaboration among stakeholders involved in decision-making. With a shared understanding of each alternative, stakeholders can offer valuable input and feedback, fostering a collaborative environment where individuals contribute their perspectives and expertise, ultimately leading to more well-rounded decisions.

Furthermore, defining alternatives consistently enhances transparency and accountability. When decision-makers articulate the traits and characteristics of each alternative, tracing the decision back to its original intent becomes easier. This increased transparency not only improves the decision-making process but also holds decision-makers accountable for their choices.

Establishing clear criteria and metrics for evaluation is essential to ensure a consistent and clear definition of alternatives. Criteria should be *specific, measurable, attainable, relevant, and time-bound (SMART)*. Utilizing such criteria enables decision-makers to objectively assess each alternative and compare them against one another, reducing ambiguity, increasing clarity, and facilitating effective decision-making.

Comprehensive and Mutually Exclusive

A well-rounded alternative encompasses all pertinent aspects and factors related to the decision. It accounts for diverse perspectives, considerations, and potential outcomes, thoroughly examining every possibility. This comprehensive approach allows for more in-depth evaluation and analysis, empowering decision-makers to make well-informed choices.

Another essential characteristic of a good alternative is mutual exclusivity. This feature guarantees that the considered alternatives are distinct and non-overlapping, meaning each option presents a unique solution or approach to the problem. By offering diverse pathways and options, mutually exclusive alternatives enable decision-makers to explore various scenarios and possibilities. Consequently, this allows for a more comprehensive comparison and assessment of each alternative's pros and cons, leading to better-informed decision-making.

The fusion of comprehensiveness and mutual exclusivity in alternatives establishes a solid foundation for decision-making. As such, it considers all relevant factors and perspectives, addressing every critical aspect. This holistic approach enables decision-makers to grasp the situation fully and make informed choices, considering all potential implications.

Moreover, mutually exclusive alternatives ensure decision-makers have distinct options, eliminating redundancy and repetition. This distinction streamlines analysis, making weighing each alternative's pros and cons and effectively comparing them simpler.

Additionally, comprehensive and mutually exclusive alternatives foster creativity and innovation in decision-making. By examining various options and considering various possibilities, decision-makers can break free from conventional thinking and uncover innovative solutions to complex problems.

Can Expose Fundamental Tradeoffs

A good alternative is characterized not only by its positive features but also by the necessary concessions and compromises it entails. Exploring these tradeoffs provides valuable insights into our decisions' true nature and implications. Remember that life seldom offers simple, black-and-white choices; instead, we must navigate a complex landscape where each alternative presents its own set of consequences.

By acknowledging the tradeoffs inherent in good alternatives, we avoid oversimplified decision-making. This approach urges us to delve deeper and critically evaluate the potential costs, risks, and sacrifices that could accompany our chosen path. This awareness enables us to make choices aligned with our priorities and long-term goals rather than being influenced by short-term gains or superficial appeal.

Furthermore, grasping fundamental tradeoffs equips us with a more realistic and balanced approach to decision-making. It cultivates a mindset of acceptance, understanding that perfection is often unattainable, and pursuing it may result in paralysis or missed opportunities. Instead, we learn to assess alternatives based on comprehensive knowledge of their pros and cons, weighing them against our preferences and circumstances.

Developed Collaboratively With Those Affected

An alternative that is developed collaboratively with those affected is a powerful tool for finding the best solutions. The alternative can be tailored to meet each stakeholder's unique needs and preferences by involving all relevant parties in the decision-making process.

This approach promotes buy-in, ownership, and shared account-ability, leading to more successful outcomes and better stakeholder relationships. When everyone has a say in the development of the alternative, the likelihood of unexpected challenges or conflicts arising down the line decreases significantly. A collaborative approach is more likely to achieve outcomes than one involving only one individual or group.

As you consider different solution alternatives, also recognize that existing solutions may have been tried and tested. Recognizing and utilizing known solutions can save you time, reduce costs and improve the likelihood of success in solving a problem.

Previous Solutions for the Same Problem

Examining previous solutions for recurring problems can yield valuable insights and lessons for effective decision-making. Analyzing past approaches allows us to learn from others' successes and failures, broadening our perspective and laying the groundwork for innovative strategies.

One method to discover previous solutions is through **historical analysis**. Investigating history helps us uncover how individuals, organizations, or societies have addressed similar challenges. By studying their methods and outcomes, we can gain inspiration and draw upon the wisdom of those who faced comparable situations.

Besides historical analysis, it is essential to **explore contemporary solutions**. Evaluating recent attempts to address the same problem offer a glimpse into the current landscape. This examination enables us to identify emerging trends, novel approaches, and potential breakthroughs that more effectively tackle the issue.

Another resource to consider is the **insights shared by experts and thought leaders**. Accessing their perspectives through books, articles, interviews, or conferences can provide a wealth of knowledge. Experts often share experiences, best practices, and innovative strategies that successfully address the problem. By absorbing their wisdom, we can incorporate their insights into our decision-making process and potentially refine or adapt solutions to fit our unique circumstances.

Furthermore, **examining firsthand experiences and perspectives** of those who have faced similar challenges can be invaluable. Engaging with individuals or organizations who have confronted the same problem through conversations, interviews, or case studies allows us to understand various solutions' nuances, contextual factors, and practical implications. Their firsthand accounts offer real-world insights and serve as a valuable source of information for shaping our decision-making approach.

However, recognize that each problem is unique, and past solutions may not be optimal for the current situation. Studying previous solutions aims to build a foundation of knowledge and inspiration for our decision-making process rather than seeking a one-size-fits-all answer. Armed with a comprehensive understanding of past approaches and their outcomes, we can creatively adapt, innovate, and tailor solutions to address the problem more effectively and impactfully.

Previously Disregarded Solutions for the Same Problem

Pursuing effective decision-making necessitates exploring previously overlooked solutions to the same problem. Often, we become trapped in a cycle of repetitive thinking, relying on familiar strategies and approaches. This limited perspective may impede our ability to uncover innovative solutions and hinder progress. By breaking away from conventional thinking, we can access a realm of untapped possibilities.

One method for discovering previously disregarded solutions is **challenging our assumptions and biases.** We all harbor preconceived notions and ingrained beliefs that can cloud our judgment. Consciously questioning these assumptions and adopting a more open-minded mindset allows alternative ideas and perspectives to surface. This change in thinking can unveil solutions previously concealed.

Additionally, **seeking inspiration from diverse sources** can catalyze the discovery of overlooked solutions. Interacting with individuals from different backgrounds, cultures, and expertise areas expands our knowledge and broadens our horizons. Actively pursuing diverse perspectives exposes us to innovative ideas and approaches that can inspire breakthrough solutions.

Another valuable tactic involves **exploring unrelated fields and disciplines**. Venturing outside our specific problem domain enables us to draw inspiration from seemingly unrelated industries or areas of study. Concepts and practices from other fields can provide fresh insights and novel approaches adaptable to our challenges. This interdisciplinary exploration can ignite creativity and lead to unexpected breakthroughs.

Furthermore, **revisiting past attempts and failures** can offer valuable insights. Solutions discarded in the past may hold hidden potential or instructive lessons. Examining previous approaches with a fresh perspective allows us to identify overlooked aspects or new ways to leverage those ideas. Lessons learned from past failures can guide us toward alternative paths and solutions previously dismissed.

Alternatives for a Similar Problem

One method for discovering alternatives involves drawing inspiration from similar situations or cases. Examine examples from your own experiences or others that share parallels with the problem. Studying how others have addressed similar challenges can provide insights and ideas applicable to your situation, allowing you to access a wealth of knowledge and learn from others' successes and failures.

Another strategy for generating alternatives is engaging in brainstorming or idea-generation sessions. Assemble a diverse group of individuals with varying backgrounds and perspectives to explore potential solutions collaboratively. Foster open and non-judgmental discussions, creating an environment where creativity flourishes. Unique alternatives that may not have been initially apparent can be uncovered by harnessing the group's collective wisdom.

Moreover, consider utilizing technology and data-driven approaches to reveal alternatives. Analyze relevant data sets, research, and employ tools and software that offer insights and generate alternative scenarios. This data-driven approach can help identify patterns, trends, and possible options previously overlooked. Combining human intuition and analysis with technological capabilities can expand your understanding and uncover innovative alternatives.

Subsequently, it is also essential to think beyond conventional approaches and challenge assumptions. Often, we default to familiar solutions without considering alternative viewpoints. Encourage yourself and others to question existing assumptions and explore unconventional paths. This can involve thinking outside the box, examining different industries or domains, or seeking inspiration from unrelated fields. By stepping outside your comfort zone, you create new opportunities for creativity and problem-solving.

Keep in mind that the objective is to generate a diverse array of alternatives for objective evaluation. Each alternative should be assessed based on feasibility, potential impact, and alignment with your goals and values. Thoroughly examining and considering multiple alternatives increases the likelihood of finding an effective solution and making a well-informed decision.

Generating Creative Alternatives

Embrace thinking outside the box when considering alternatives. While some options may initially seem like poor choices, a closer examination can reveal their viability as we gain a deeper understanding. To pursue suitable alternatives, whether good or seemingly bad, ask yourself the following questions:

- What are my alternative courses of action?
- Are there potentially good alternatives not on the list?
- Which alternatives have I missed that others might consider?
- Who could help me create better alternatives?
- Do my alternatives take into account those I care about?
- Do my alternatives appear to form a complete set?
- What other alternatives should I consider?
- What might someone I trust and admire do?

Brainstorming can be more effective when examining alternatives by first answering questions personally and then as part of a group. However, never assume that there are no alternatives and avoid placing limits on potential options.

Remember that different ideas are entirely acceptable. If you require detailed information to make a decision and ask specific questions, you are on the right track. Consider how a scene can appear entirely different when viewed from various angles. Keep this in mind as we explore perspectives and options from different viewpoints in the next chapter.

Chapter 7:
Look From Different Angles

Imagine a kaleidoscope where the colors and shapes shift and blend uniquely whenever you turn it. Just like a kaleidoscope, when it comes to problem-solving, shifting our perspective can reveal new options and possibilities that we may have never considered. This chapter will explore how looking at problems from different angles and perspectives can help us identify new and innovative solutions.

Tools

The wrong tools for a task can render it nearly impossible to complete. When it comes to decision-making, we must equip ourselves with the necessary tools, as discussed below.

Brainstorming

Brainstorming, engaging in conversations, creating wish lists, and employing creative methods are all potent tools for identifying new and unique perspectives on a problem. Utilizing these tools can provide fresh insights and enable the development of innovative solutions that may not have been apparent otherwise.

Through brainstorming, the power of human imagination can be harnessed in a creative process that encourages the free flow of ideas and concepts. In essence, a brainstorming session involves a group of people gathering to share suggestions, with one person documenting them, ideally on a whiteboard. Once the group has exhausted their ideas, it is time to discuss the recorded suggestions, eliminating those deemed unworkable and ultimately converging on the most suitable option.

Conversations With Others

Discussions can generate new perspectives and ideas on a particular problem or challenge. Diversifying our ideas by interacting with diverse individuals is a useful decision-making tool. Different perspectives allow us to gain valuable insights that we may not have considered before.

The key to productive conversations is approaching them with an open mind and a willingness to listen and learn. If we are alert and engaged, asking questions as the conversation unfolds can help us better understand an issue.

Also, conversations with others can help to identify blind spots in our thinking and challenge our assumptions, leading to more comprehensive and effective solutions. However, it is important to be mindful of potential biases or limitations in the perspectives of those we speak with. It can be helpful to seek out diverse viewpoints and to critically evaluate the information presented to ensure that it is relevant and reliable. When done effectively, conversations with others can be a powerful tool for generating creative and innovative solutions to complex problems.

Wish Lists

Wish lists can be a powerful tool for generating fresh ideas and unique perspectives. As the name suggests, wish lists involve compiling a list of desirable outcomes or ideal solutions to a particular problem. This exercise encourages individuals to think beyond the limitations of practicality and feasibility and focus on the underlying desires or needs that drive their decision-making.

When you create a list of wishes, you can highlight priorities and discover new ways to achieve your objectives. Likewise, it allows for a collaborative effort, as individuals can share their wish lists with others and build upon each other's ideas.

Creativity Methods

Creativity is a skill, and creativity methods are powerful tools that can bring about *"out of the box"* options. These methods can take many forms, such as mind mapping, lateral thinking, or the *SCAMPER method (Substitute, Combine, Adapt, Modify, Put to another use, Eliminate, Reverse).*

Creative methods allow you to approach a problem or challenge from an entirely new angle. By doing so, you can free yourself from traditional ways of looking at problems and come up with many new solutions. These methods can also help you identify unexpected connections between seemingly unrelated ideas. In turn, they can lead to truly innovative and original solutions.

Moreover, it can be entertaining and enjoyable. They often involve playful or imaginative activities that can help stimulate your creativity and bring a sense of playfulness to the problem-solving process.

Engaging in these activities can help you tap into your inner child and unlock new sources of creativity.

What to Look For

Having a clear understanding of what to look for is crucial in decision-making. This involves identifying key factors and considerations relevant to the decision, enabling you to gather information, evaluate options, and make informed choices.

Associated Costs

Associated costs are essential to decision-making, including financial and non-financial implications. Consider monetary expenses like upfront costs, maintenance, hidden fees, and non-financial costs such as time commitments, resource allocation, and potential trade-offs. Understanding the full scope of associated costs allows for a realistic evaluation of a decision's feasibility and its impact on resources.

Risks

Every decision carries risks, which must be evaluated and understood. Identifying potential risks enables you to assess the likelihood of negative outcomes and develop mitigation strategies. Analyze factors like uncertainty, volatility, obstacles, and stakeholder impacts to make calculated decisions and prepare for challenges.

For example, investing in the stock market requires assessing risks like market volatility, economic conditions, and company-specific risks. Understanding these risks informs decisions on portfolio diversification, risk tolerance, and mitigation strategies.

Trade-Offs

Trade-offs are inevitable in decision-making and involve sacrificing aspects or benefits in exchange for others. Consider trade-offs associated with different options by weighing advantages and disadvantages, prioritizing objectives, and understanding potential consequences. Conscious and informed trade-offs align decisions with goals and maximize overall value.

Suppose you weigh a decision in accepting a job offer in another city. As such, it requires considering career advancement and new opportunities against leaving friends and family, adjusting to a new environment, and lifestyle changes. Understanding trade-offs helps prioritize what matters most, leading to a decision that aligns with long-term aspirations.

Benefits

Effective decision-making offers numerous advantages for both individuals and organizations. By making well-informed choices, personal and professional lives can be improved in various ways. First, decision-making allows us to achieve our goals and aspirations more accurately by carefully considering alternatives and evaluating potential outcomes. Second, it empowers us to take control of our lives, shaping our desired future and fostering a sense of agency and autonomy. Furthermore, informed decisions promote personal growth and development as each choice is a learning opportunity, refining critical thinking skills, judgment, and problem-solving abilities. Ultimately, effective decision-making enhances overall well-being and fulfillment, leading to a more purposeful and successful life.

Probability of Success

The quality of decisions directly influences the likelihood of success. Informed choices involve careful evaluation of information, risk and benefit consideration, and realistic situation assessment. By thoroughly analyzing influencing factors, uncertainties can be minimized, and calculated steps toward success can be taken. Informed decision-making enables capitalizing on opportunities that align with goals and values, identifying promising options, strategically allocating resources, and optimizing efforts. While success is never guaranteed, the probability of achieving positive outcomes significantly increases with thorough, clear, and long-term goal-focused decision-making.

Impact

Every decision carries an impact, affecting our lives and those around us. It is essential to recognize the potential consequences of decisions and act responsibly. Decisions shape personal and professional relationships, career paths, and overall well-being. In organizational contexts, decisions can have far-reaching effects on teams, stakeholders, and society. Understanding potential consequences helps navigate ethical dilemmas, anticipate unintended outcomes, and align decisions with values and broader societal interests. By acknowledging the impact of decisions, decision-making can be approached with greater mindfulness, empathy, and a sense of social responsibility.

There are four questions that we can ask ourselves to simplify our understanding of the severity of the impact. Those questions are as follows:

- *Will the effect be felt immediately or gradually over time?*

- *Is it limited to a specific area, or will it have wide-ranging consequences?*

- *Are there options for reversing the effect if needed?*

- *Will the impact greatly affect the success or failure of the decision?*

What to Avoid

Effective decision-making requires awareness of potential pitfalls that hinder making informed choices. Recognizing and avoiding these pitfalls enhances decision-making and increases the likelihood of achieving desirable outcomes. Here are key factors to consider:

Assuming No Alternatives Exist

Thinking that no alternatives exist can constrain our perspective and inhibit optimal decision-making. Adopting an open mindset and actively seeking alternative options unlocks new possibilities and reveals innovative solutions. Embracing the notion of existing alternatives allows for exploring different paths, challenging conventional thinking, and discovering creative problem-solving approaches. This mindset shift enables us to broaden our horizons and make decisions that foster growth and success.

Navigating Many Alternatives

At times, a multitude of alternatives can overwhelm us and obstruct the decision-making process. When confronted with numerous options or minor variations, focusing on priorities, goals, values, and desired outcomes is necessary. Evaluating each alternative based on relevance and potential impact helps filter out distractions and minor variations that may steer us away from core decisions. Simplifying the decision landscape facilitates more efficient and effective choices, liberating us from analysis paralysis and guiding us toward desired results.

Considering Alternatives That Are Not Doable

Investigating seemingly unattainable alternatives might appear counter-intuitive. However, it can be beneficial for expanding our thinking and discovering innovative solutions. While these alternatives may not be immediately viable, they can inspire new insights and ideas. Entertaining seemingly impossible options challenges current thinking limitations and fosters a mindset of possibility. This approach encourages out-of-the-box thinking, enhanced creativity, and the discovery of novel strategies that may eventually lead to achievable alternatives. Embracing the exploration of seemingly unattainable options paves the way for unconventional solutions and potential breakthroughs exceeding initial expectations.

Accepting Unnecessary Limits to Alternatives

Accepting unnecessary limits to alternatives can hinder decision-making, as individuals and organizations may unknowingly confine themselves to a narrow range of options. This constraint inhibits the exploration of new ideas and possibilities. Challenging preconceived notions and embracing a mindset of openness and creativity allows for considering a broader spectrum of alternatives, leading to unique solutions that might have been overlooked. Recognizing and questioning self-imposed limitations unlocks the potential for more successful and transformative decision-making.

Forgetting the "Do Nothing" Alternative

Amid the urgency to act and solve problems, maintaining the status quo can be a legitimate option that warrants careful consideration. Refraining from immediate action and further evaluating the situation is sometimes the best decision. Assessing the potential consequences of inaction and long-term implications provides a deeper understanding of the problem. The *"do nothing"* alternative is a benchmark against which other options can be measured, enabling a more informed and deliberate choice. Acknowledging the value of the *"do nothing"* alternative helps avoid hasty decisions and ensures that the chosen course of action is the most beneficial.

As aforementioned, alternatives all have some merit. Nothing needs to be left off the table regarding ideas or suggestions. If we are too reluctant to explore alternatives, we may miss a good opportunity. Brainstorming, conversations with others, and lists of other options form some of the tools you have learned in this chapter. With that in mind, we can now move forward to analyzing the data we collect to decide.

Pillar 4:
Analyze

Once all the information has been compiled, you will need to analyze what you have in front of you. There has to be some form of order and this can be arrived at through analysis. Basically, we want to break everything down into smaller parts and make assessments on each part. That way, we allow ourselves the best opportunity to make the correct decision.

Chapter 8:
Values and Goals

Our values stem from various sources, including religion, spirituality, and societal norms. Values encompass ideals and tangible aspects of our lives, such as relationships with friends and family. There is a notable relationship between values and goals; some believe values inform goals, while others argue the opposite. This discussion will explore the interplay between values and goals, examining their positive and negative influences on decision-making.

Defining Your Values and Goals

Establishing your values and goals is a crucial step in the decision-making process. Gaining a clear understanding of what matters to you and the aspirations you aim to achieve lays a solid foundation for choices that align with your true self. Clarifying your values and goals fosters a sense of direction and purpose, enabling decisions that contribute to overall fulfillment and success.

Values act as guiding principles shaping your beliefs, attitudes, and behaviors. They reflect the importance you place on certain aspects of life and provide a moral compass for decision-making. For instance, valuing honesty and integrity influences choices that uphold these principles. Identifying values requires self-reflection and introspection, considering the qualities and ideals you cherish and the person you aspire to be.

Conversely, goals are specific objectives aimed at achieving various life aspects. They offer a roadmap for decision-making, guiding desired outcomes. Defining goals necessitates making them *specific, measurable, achievable, relevant, and time-bound (SMART)*. For example, advancing your career might involve setting a SMART goal of obtaining a managerial position within two years.

The importance of defining values and goals is exemplified by a hypothetical situation involving two job opportunities: one with a higher salary but compromising work-life balance and another with a lower salary offering flexibility and personal pursuit time. By previously defining values and goals, the assessment of which opportunity aligns better with values and contributes to long-term goals becomes clearer. In this case, if work-life balance and personal fulfillment are essential, the latter option may be chosen despite the lower salary.

Defining values and goals creates a framework guiding the decision-making process, helping prioritize what matters and filtering out choices that deviate from the intended path. It also empowers focus and decisions that bring you closer to long-term aspirations. Remember that values and goals are personal and unique to each individual. Invest time in introspection, identifying values, and setting meaningful goals that serve as beacons in your decision-making journey.

Defining the Ideal Situation and Alternatives

Envisioning the desired result creates a target to guide your decision-making process, determining success and establishing specific criteria defining the ideal state.

Begin by reflecting on your goals, aspirations, and values underpinning your decision. Contemplate the specific outcomes you hope to attain and key factors contributing to your vision of success. For example, in a career change scenario, an ideal situation might involve a fulfilling job aligned with your passions, offering growth and development opportunities. Defining this ideal scenario provides clarity, enabling decisions that move you closer to the desired outcome.

With a clear understanding of the ideal situation, explore and evaluate alternatives, representing different paths or options available for achieving the desired outcome. These can range from simple choices to complex strategies, each having advantages and disadvantages.

Then, brainstorm various alternatives, evaluating their feasibility, benefits, and potential risks. For instance, consider alternatives such as beach resorts, adventure-filled excursions, or cultural explorations when deciding on a vacation destination. Considering multiple options broadens your perspective and opens up unique experiences and possibilities.

Subsequently, assess each alternative based on its alignment with the defined ideal situation. Analyze how well each option fulfills the desired outcome, meets criteria, and aligns with values and priorities. Evaluating alternatives against these factors enables more informed decisions resonating with aspirations.

Additionally, note that alternatives are not limited to mutually exclusive choices. In some cases, combining elements from multiple alternatives can create innovative and customized solutions, leading to a tailored approach maximizing the benefits and minimizing each option's drawbacks.

Defining the ideal situation and exploring alternatives provides a clearer understanding of what you truly want and the options to achieve it. This empowers decision-making aligned with your vision of success, increasing the likelihood of positive outcomes and personal fulfillment. Remember, decision-making is not solely about choosing between options but shaping your path toward a future aligning with values, aspirations, and unique circumstances.

Chapter 9:
Risk Analysis

Evaluating the risks linked to the *"best"* solution is vital to the decision-making process. While we might be tempted to concentrate solely on a specific choice's advantages and potential rewards, it's crucial to acknowledge that every decision entails inherent risks. Comprehending and assessing these risks allow us to make more informed and well-rounded decisions.

Risk assessment aims to confirm that the selected solution aligns with our overarching goals and objectives. Although a solution may seem ideal at first glance, scrutinizing the related risks might expose potential downsides or adverse consequences that could obstruct our progress or impede long-term success. By considering these risks, we can conduct a more extensive evaluation of the solution's appropriateness and determine if it corresponds with our intended outcomes.

Additionally, evaluating risks enables us to anticipate and prepare for possible challenges or setbacks. No decision is devoid of uncertainties and potential pitfalls. Proactively identifying and analyzing the involved risks allows us to devise contingency plans and strategies to reduce or minimize their effects. This forward-thinking approach furnishes us with the necessary tools and resources to address potential hurdles and enhances our capacity to adapt and respond effectively.

For instance, consider a business contemplating a significant expansion into a new market. While the prospects for growth and profitability might be alluring, assessing the risks accompanying this expansion is required. This could involve examining factors such as market volatility, regulatory shifts, the competitive landscape, and potential financial risks. By thoroughly evaluating these risks, the business can make an informed decision about whether to proceed and, if so, create strategies to mitigate the identified risks, such as diversifying their product offerings or conducting in-depth market research.

Furthermore, risk assessment offers a pragmatic perspective on the potential trade-offs involved in a decision. It assists us in weighing the possible benefits against the potential drawbacks, enabling us to make informed choices based on a balanced assessment of the overall impact. By recognizing the risks, we can sidestep unquestioning optimism or excessively positive evaluations that could result in poor decision-making.

Steps To Conduct a Risk Analysis

By performing an in-depth risk analysis, we can gain a more profound understanding of the possible consequences and uncertainties, empowering us to make well-informed decisions. Below are the steps in conducting risk analysis.

Risk Identification

Risk identification entails systematically recognizing and documenting potential risks that may emerge during the execution of a decision. It necessitates thoroughly examining internal and external factors that could influence the intended outcomes. This stage is critical because it helps us foresee and prepare for potential obstacles and challenges.

To effectively identify risks, involving relevant stakeholders with knowledge and expertise in the subject is crucial. Facilitating brainstorming sessions, interviews, or surveys can foster a collaborative approach to risk identification. Establishing a safe and open environment that encourages participants to express their viewpoints and bring up potential risks without fear of judgment is essential.

During the risk identification phase, categorizing risks into different types ensures comprehensive coverage. For instance, strategic risks might stem from shifts in market trends or competitor actions, while operational risks could result from process failures or resource limitations. Financial risks may encompass budget overruns or revenue fluctuations, and compliance risks could emerge from legal or regulatory changes.

To exemplify the process, let us consider a scenario. Suppose you are a project manager responsible for developing a new software application. During risk identification, you assemble your team and conduct a brainstorming session to pinpoint potential risks. The team identifies risks such as delays in software development, inadequate testing, data security breaches, and unforeseen changes in user requirements. By classifying and documenting these risks, you can develop a comprehensive understanding of the potential challenges that may arise throughout the project

Risk Estimation

Risk estimation involves assessing potential risks linked to various options or actions. It enables us to determine the probability and impact of uncertain outcomes, allowing us to make more informed choices. Effective risk estimation necessitates a systematic approach considering historical data, expert opinions, and qualitative evaluations.

Accurate risk estimation requires gathering pertinent information and analyzing it meticulously. For instance, when contemplating investing in a specific stock, you would scrutinize the company's financial performance, industry trends, and market conditions. By examining past performance and understanding potential risks, like market volatility or regulatory shifts, you can make a more informed decision about the investment.

Quantitative methods, including statistical analysis and modeling, can also assist in risk estimation. Assigning probabilities to different results and conducting scenario analyses allows us to quantify potential risks and their impacts. For example, a project manager might employ Monte Carlo simulation to evaluate the likelihood of meeting project deadlines based on resource availability, task dependencies, and uncertainties in estimating effort.

Besides quantitative approaches, qualitative assessments play a vital role in risk estimation. This involves considering subjective factors and expert judgments. In healthcare decision-making, for example, experts may assess the risks associated with a new treatment by examining potential side effects, patient demographics, and clinical trial outcomes. These qualitative assessments offer valuable insights and complement quantitative analyses.

A significant aspect of risk estimation is acknowledging the relationship between risks and potential rewards. High-risk options may yield greater potential rewards, while low-risk options provide more stability but limited returns. Comprehending this trade-off is essential for making risk-informed decisions. An entrepreneur evaluating diverse business ventures must, for example, assess the potential risks involved, such as market competition and financial viability, to determine which opportunity aligns with their risk tolerance and long-term objectives.

In conclusion, risk estimation equips us to make decisions with a comprehensive understanding of uncertainties and potential outcomes.

Risk Perception

Risk perception can differ significantly among individuals and may be influenced by various factors. Cognitive biases are one such factor. These inherent mental shortcuts that our brains employ when processing information can lead to systematic errors in judgment. For instance, the heuristic availability bias prompts us to overestimate the likelihood of easily recalled events, like plane crashes, while underestimating more frequent risks, such as car accidents. Acknowledging and being aware of these biases can make more rational and objective risk assessments.

Moreover, our past experiences and personal beliefs significantly shape our risk perception. For example, someone with a negative experience related to a certain activity or investment might perceive it as riskier than someone without such an experience. Likewise, cultural and societal influences can mold our risk perception, as different cultures may have varying attitudes toward specific risks, affecting how individuals perceive and respond to them.

Furthermore, how risks are communicated and framed can substantially impact our perception. Presenting information, vivid language usage, and the context in which risks are depicted can all influence our perception of their severity and likelihood. This is evident in marketing, where advertisers often employ fear appeals to manipulate consumers' perception of risks associated with not using their products or services.

It is crucial to recognize that risk perception is not solely based on objective data or facts; it is a subjective process influenced by emotions, biases, experiences, and societal factors. By becoming aware of these influences, we can aim for a more balanced and accurate risk assessment.

In decision-making, comprehending risk perception can help us make more informed choices. By considering how different individuals or groups perceive risks, we can effectively tailor our communication strategies to convey potential risks and benefits. Additionally, acknowledging our biases and mitigating their influence can result in more objective risk assessments.

Ultimately, risk perception plays a critical role in decision-making, shaping our understanding of uncertainties and guiding our choices. By exploring the intricacies of risk perception, we can better understand how it impacts our decision-making processes and strive for more informed and rational decision-making.

Risk Evaluation

Risk evaluation is a crucial element of the decision-making process, enabling us to assess potential risks linked to various options or actions. Through thorough risk assessment, we can make informed decisions that optimize opportunities and minimize possible adverse outcomes.

For effective risk evaluation, identify and analyze the potential consequences and likelihood of each risk occurrence. This involves examining the immediate and long-term impacts a risk may have on our goals, resources, and stakeholders. For instance, suppose you are contemplating starting a new business venture. In the risk evaluation phase, you would assess potential risks such as financial losses, market competition, regulatory compliance, and operational challenges. By meticulously examining the potential consequences and likelihood of these risks, you can make a more informed decision on whether to proceed and, if so, how to effectively mitigate those risks.

Another vital aspect of risk evaluation is considering the risk tolerance and risk appetite of the decision-maker or organization. Risk tolerance refers to the degree of risk one is willing to accept, while risk appetite denotes the amount of risk one is prepared to take in pursuit of their objectives. Various aspects, including personal values, organizational culture, financial capacity, and the nature of the decision, influence these factors. For example, a conservative investor may have lower risk tolerance and prefer safer investment options. In comparison, a more aggressive investor may have higher risk tolerance and be willing to embrace greater risks for potentially higher returns. Understanding your risk tolerance and appetite helps align your decisions with your comfort level and desired outcomes.

During the risk evaluation process, consider the potential mitigating measures or risk management strategies that can be implemented. These strategies aim to decrease the likelihood or impact of identified risks. As such, if you are considering investing in the stock market, you may diversify your portfolio to mitigate the risk of concentrating all your assets in one area. By evaluating risks and identifying appropriate risk management strategies, you can proactively address potential challenges and enhance the overall success of your decision.

As we transition to the next pillar, recall that we have just examined the necessity for analysis and the specific aspects that warrant scrutiny. While several methods are available, once you have completed your detailed analysis and are prepared to decide, the situation becomes more tangible. You must stand by your decision and take action. Your comprehension of the factual components required for decision-making shapes the journey leading to the decision. However, a new journey commences after making the decision—one focused on practicality and implementation, which we will delve into in-depth under the next pillar.

Pillar 5:
Implement

After completing your analysis, we need to implement the sum of what we have arrived at. Implementation can be quite a delicate task, and it is quite acceptable to take our time. We want to ensure that we are proceeding in the most effective way by putting our decisions into practice.

Chapter 10:
The Action Plan

The well-known adage, often attributed to Benjamin Franklin, states that *"failing to plan is planning to fail."* While the phrase might seem cliché, it holds a substantial truth. Approaching any situation without a well-defined action plan can significantly reduce the likelihood of success. Although some may thrive in spontaneous situations, we aim to make sound decisions based on a reliable plan guiding our actions. In Pillar 4, we explored the importance of analysis and gathering comprehensive information to make informed decisions. This process allowed us to eliminate unfavorable options, identify viable alternatives, and streamline the decision-making process effectively. Similarly, our plan must possess these qualities. In this chapter, we will delve into the concept of a plan, discuss its significance in greater detail, and provide guidance on creating a solid plan.

What Is an Action Plan?

An action plan is an indispensable instrument that converts decisions into practical steps. It acts as a roadmap, outlining the tasks, timelines, and resources required to accomplish desired goals. Consider it the blueprint for turning your decisions into tangible outcomes, providing clarity and direction that enables you to navigate the path toward success effectively.

To emphasize the importance of an action plan, let us examine an example. Suppose you decide to start a new business. Without an action plan, this decision may remain a mere concept with no clear way forward. However, crafting a well-structured action plan can break down the process into manageable tasks. Your action plan might include conducting market research, defining your target audience, securing funding, devising a marketing strategy, and establishing a timeline for each task. This plan provides a coherent roadmap to guide your actions and ensure progress toward your entrepreneurial goals.

An action plan offers several key advantages. First, it helps maintain organization and focus by breaking down complex decisions into smaller, achievable tasks. Outlining specific actions prevents feeling overwhelmed. Second, an action plan facilitates resource allocation. By identifying necessary resources, such as finances, time, and personnel, you can allocate them efficiently to optimize productivity and minimize roadblocks. Third, an action plan is a monitoring tool, enabling you to track progress and adjust as needed. It ensures you stay on course and implements corrective actions if deviations occur.

Developing an effective action plan entails incorporating several steps, including:

Make a List of Actions

Developing a list of actions is an effective strategy in the decision-making process. After identifying your options and evaluating their advantages and disadvantages, it is crucial to determine the specific steps required to execute your decision efficiently. Listing the necessary actions brings clarity and structure to the decision-making process, transforming abstract concepts into tangible plans.

To create a list of actions, begin by breaking down your decision into smaller, manageable tasks. Consider the essential milestones or stages to be accomplished along the way. For instance, if your decision involves starting a new business, your list may include tasks such as conducting market research, devising a business plan, securing funding, and formulating a marketing strategy. Breaking down the decision into actionable steps provides a clear roadmap to follow.

Ensure that each action on your list is specific, measurable, and time-bound. This entails defining a clear outcome, a method to track progress, and a deadline for completing each task. Instead of listing an ambiguous action like *"Research potential suppliers,"* specify it as *"Identify and contact at least five potential suppliers by the end of the week."* This level of specificity promotes accountability and enables effective progress tracking.

Moreover, prioritize your list of actions based on their importance and dependencies. Recognize tasks that must be completed before others can commence. This approach helps establish a logical sequence and ensures smooth progression toward achieving your goal. By comprehending the dependencies between actions, you can allocate time and resources efficiently.

As you work through your list, mark off completed tasks and acknowledge your progress. This sense of accomplishment fuels momentum and encourages you to continue moving forward.

Set SMART Goals

A fundamental aspect of effective decision-making is setting SMART goals. SMART, an acronym for specific, measurable, achievable, relevant, and time-bound, is a framework that enables the creation of clear and actionable goals to enhance the decision-making process.

First, goals should be **specific**, meaning they must be well-defined and precise, eliminating ambiguity. A specific goal, such as *"increase sales by 10% within the next quarter,"* is preferable to a vague one like "improve sales." The more specific your goal, the easier it is to make decisions aligned with its achievement.

Second, goals should be **measurable**, requiring the establishment of metrics or indicators to track progress. For example, if your goal is to *"improve customer satisfaction,"* set a measurable goal like *"increase customer satisfaction ratings from 80% to 90% in six months."* Measurable goals allowed for progress assessment and informed decision-making based on tangible data.

Third, goals should be **achievable**, balancing ambition with possibility. Setting unattainable goals can result in frustration and demotivation. When setting achievable goals, consider available resources, skills, and external factors. For instance, instead of an unrealistic goal like *"achieving 100% market share within a month"* for a new product launch, aim to *"capture 10% of the target market within the first quarter."*

Fourth, goals should be **relevant**, aligning with overall objectives and decision-making needs. Each goal should contribute to the bigger picture and facilitate progress toward desired outcomes. For example, if your objective is international business expansion, a relevant goal might be *"improve language proficiency in the target market."*

Lastly, goals should be **time-bound**, establishing a timeframe for achievement. Setting deadlines fosters urgency, helping prioritize tasks and make timely decisions. Instead of merely aiming to "increase website traffic," *a time-bound goal could be "increase website traffic by 20% within three months."*

By setting SMART goals, you create a framework that guides the decision-making process, maintaining focus, measuring progress, and making informed choices aligned with desired outcomes. The power of SMART goals lies in their ability to transform abstract aspirations into concrete targets that drive decision-making forward.

Get the Resources Needed

Ensuring that you have the necessary resources is essential when making important decisions. These resources can take various forms, such as information, expertise, tools, and support networks. Effectively acquiring and leveraging these resources can enhance the decision-making process's quality and increase the likelihood of achieving successful outcomes.

A key resource to acquire is relevant information, which involves gathering data, conducting research, and seeking insights from reliable sources. As such, obtaining financial reports, industry analyses, and expert opinions can provide a comprehensive understanding of the company's performance and prospects if you are considering investing in a particular company. Access to this information equips you with valuable insights, guiding your decision-making in a more informed and strategic manner.

Besides information, seeking others' expertise can significantly impact the decision-making process. Consulting subject matter experts, mentors, or trusted advisors can provide valuable perspectives and insights that may not have been considered otherwise. Suppose you are a business owner contemplating expanding into new markets. Having advice from experienced entrepreneurs who have successfully navigated similar challenges can offer invaluable guidance. Their expertise can help assess risks, identify potential opportunities, and make sound decisions aligned with your business goals.

Moreover, having the right tools and resources can streamline the decision-making process. These tools can vary, depending on the decision's nature. For example, project management software can help organize, track progress, and ensure timely completion when planning a project with multiple tasks and deadlines. Utilizing such tools can improve efficiency, minimize errors, and enable better-informed decisions based on accurate and up-to-date information.

Lastly, establishing a robust support network can provide the emotional and practical support required to navigate complex decisions. This network can comprise friends, colleagues, mentors, or professional communities. When faced with challenging decisions, a supportive group offering guidance, encouragement, and diverse perspectives can be invaluable. They can supply feedback, challenge assumptions, and help consider alternative viewpoints, ultimately enhancing the decision-making process's overall quality.

Set a Timeline

Establishing a timeline is an essential aspect of the decision-making process. A clear decision-making timeframe introduces structure and accountability, fostering focus and productivity. Timelines generate a sense of urgency, preventing the decision-making process from stagnating while facilitating resource allocation, information gathering, and outcome assessment within a specific period.

Consider the example of exploring a new career path. A timeline might include milestones such as researching industries and job roles within a month, networking and conducting informational interviews within two months, and finalizing the decision with an action plan by the third month. Breaking down the decision-making process into distinct timeframes promotes momentum and progress toward the goal.

A timeline also helps balance thoroughness and efficiency in decision-making. While gathering ample information and considering relevant factors is vital, excessive deliberation can result in analysis paralysis and lost opportunities. With a well-defined timeline, you can maintain an equilibrium between thoughtful consideration and prompt action.

Additionally, timelines facilitate risk anticipation and mitigation related to the decision. Setting interim deadlines and checkpoints allows you to evaluate progress regularly and make adjustments if needed. This proactive approach enables early identification and resolution of challenges or obstacles, ensuring you stay on course toward the final decision.

Lastly, timelines should be realistic and flexible. Factors such as decision complexity, information availability, and external circumstances may necessitate adjustments. Likewise, remain adaptable and revise your timeline as required while preserving a sense of urgency and purpose.

Track Your Progress

Monitoring progress is a vital component of effective decision-making. It facilitates the evaluation of decision outcomes, assessment of their effectiveness, and implementation of necessary adjustments. Maintaining a record of your progress offers valuable insights into decision-making patterns, ultimately enhancing future choices.

Measuring progress allows for a tangible assessment of decision impact. It reveals actual results and outcomes, indicating whether they align with initial expectations. For instance, if you implement a new marketing strategy for your business, tracking progress enables analysis of key metrics such as increased website traffic, higher conversion rates, or improved customer engagement. This data helps evaluate decision effectiveness and promotes informed adjustments to optimize future marketing efforts.

Moreover, consistent progress tracking uncovers patterns and trends over time. By regularly monitoring decisions and outcomes, you can identify recurring themes, successes, and areas requiring improvement. This information empowers the refinement of the decision-making process and the ability to make better-informed choices moving forward. Recognizing which projects consistently yield positive results while others underperform allows for focus adjustment and resource allocation, maximizing success potential.

Tracking progress also establishes a valuable feedback loop, enabling learning from successes and failures and transforming them into growth and development opportunities. Reflecting on progress helps pinpoint factors contributing to positive outcomes and replicate those strategies in similar situations. Conversely, analyzing setbacks' causes and adjusting the approach accordingly creates a cycle of continuous improvement and enhances decision-making skills.

Effectively tracking progress necessitates clear and measurable goals and benchmarks for assessing progress and evaluating decision success. Technology and data analysis tools can also simplify tracking and analysis, allowing for more accurate and insightful evaluations.

The following steps help measure outcomes, identify patterns, learn from successes and failures, and refine decision-making. By adopting a systematic approach to creating an action plan, you can make data-driven adjustments, optimize decision-making, and achieve greater success in personal and professional pursuits.

Chapter 11:
Address Risks During Implementation

The decision-making journey extends beyond the initial choice, as the implementation phase is where actions bring the decision to fruition. As such, challenges and risks may emerge during this stage, and addressing them effectively is essential for successful execution and realizing desired outcomes.

Monitoring Actions

A critical aspect of managing risks during implementation is action monitoring. This involves closely observing the progress of decision execution, tracking key indicators, and evaluating whether intended outcomes are materializing. Active monitoring enables the identification of deviations, bottlenecks, or unforeseen obstacles that could impede the implementation process.

For example, consider a business launching a new product in the market. During the implementation phase, they establish a comprehensive monitoring system to track factors such as production timelines, marketing campaigns, and customer feedback. Through this monitoring process, they discover a production delay due to a supplier issue. By promptly recognizing this risk, they mitigate the delay by sourcing an alternative supplier, ensuring minimal impact on the product launch timeline.

Monitoring actions not only aids in risk identification but also fosters proactive decision-making. It offers valuable insights that facilitate timely adjustments and adaptations, keeping the implementation on course. Addressing risks swiftly minimizes potential adverse consequences and enhances the likelihood of successful outcomes.

Preventative or Acceleration Actions

In decision-making, two distinct action types can significantly impact our path to success: *preventative actions and acceleration actions*. Both are essential for shaping the outcomes of our choices and optimizing our decision-making process.

Preventative actions refer to proactive measures designed to mitigate potential risks or problems that may emerge. These actions involve identifying and addressing underlying issues before they escalate and impede progress. Implementing preventative actions aims to minimize negative consequences and protect the decision-making process.

For instance, consider a business owner planning a major expansion project. Before proceeding, they comprehensively analyze the market, competition, and financial feasibility. This assessment helps identify potential challenges, such as changing market trends or resource insufficiency. The owner then takes preventative actions, such as diversifying product offerings, securing additional funding sources, or conducting market research to stay ahead of emerging trends. These proactive measures enhance the likelihood of successful expansion and lessen the impact of unforeseen obstacles.

Conversely, **acceleration actions** are strategic maneuvers intended to boost progress and achieve desired outcomes more rapidly. These actions involve identifying opportunities, leveraging resources, and making decisive steps to expedite success.

Returning to the business owner example, they may pinpoint opportunities to accelerate growth once the expansion project begins. Such opportunities include strategic partnerships, targeted marketing campaigns, or streamlined internal processes to increase efficiency. By implementing these acceleration actions, the business owner seeks a competitive advantage, maximizes market share, and attains their expansion goals more swiftly.

Both preventative and acceleration actions serve as invaluable tools in effective decision-making. Preventive actions enable proactive risk management, while acceleration actions facilitate seizing opportunities and hastening progress. Striking a balance between these approaches is crucial, adapting actions to suit the specific context and objectives.

Conditional Actions

Integrating conditional actions into the decision-making process enables effective adaptation and response to different scenarios, enhancing the likelihood of success. As such, utilizing conditional actions involves anticipating and planning for potential obstacles or contingencies during decision implementation. This proactive mindset helps identify key conditions or triggers necessitating a change in action. Defining these conditions beforehand allows for developing alternative plans or strategies to address diverse eventualities.

Consider a business launching a new product, with decision-makers aware of volatile market conditions and rapidly changing consumer preferences. In this scenario, they incorporate conditional actions into their decision-making process, outlining specific conditions such as a sudden drop in sales or a strong competitor's emergence that would trigger a marketing strategy reassessment. As a result, they have pre-defined alternative marketing approaches and contingency plans, ensuring swift adaptation and response to changing market dynamics.

Incorporating conditional actions into decision-making fosters pre-paredness and flexibility, promoting agility in navigating unexpected challenges or shifts in circumstances and reducing potential negative impacts on desired outcomes. This approach empowers decision-making with a comprehensive understanding of potential consequences and the ability to pivot when necessary.

Subsequently, ensure conditional actions are well-thought-out and aligned with goals and values, avoiding arbitrary or reactive conditions. Instead, base them on meaningful factors with genuine impacts on decision success. By considering these conditions and developing conditional actions accordingly, adaptive decisions can be made, positioning individuals and organizations for long-term success.

Overall, in the decision-making implementation phase, three essential strategies are examined: *monitoring, preventative or acceleration, and conditional actions.* Monitoring actions highlighted the importance of actively tracking decision progress and outcomes, enabling early detection of deviations or potential issues. Furthermore, the chapter explored the significance of preventative or acceleration actions, which involve proactive measures to mitigate risks or capitalize on opportunities arising during implementation. Finally, the value of conditional actions was discussed, focusing on planning for different scenarios and adapting courses of action based on specific conditions.

Pillar 6:
Evaluate

Without evaluation, we have no means of measuring the efficacy of our decision. As we know, there are consequences to the solution to every problem. We need a way to establish the nature of the consequences. The best way to do so is by doing an evaluation informed by feedback on the outcome of the situation. That feedback then allows us to make changes if necessary.

Chapter 12:
Feedback Loop

Imagine dining at a restaurant with slow service, a less-than-perfect steak, and an elusive server when ordering drinks. It is not unusual; many people might choose not to complain out of politeness or compassion. However, without voicing concerns, managers, and owners remain unaware, and the situation remains unchanged. This exemplifies the concept of feedback or lack thereof. In any circumstance, the absence of feedback limits opportunities for change. This chapter will explore the feedback loop, its function, and methods for creating one. Additionally, it will discuss the numerous benefits of feedback loops and differentiate between positive and negative feedback loops.

What Is a Feedback Loop?

A feedback loop is a fundamental concept in decision-making, encompassing a continuous information flow and response cycle. As a self-regulating mechanism, it offers valuable input and insights to enhance the decision-making process. Feedback loops enable individuals and organizations to monitor decision outcomes, implement necessary adjustments, and foster continuous learning and adaptation.

The feedback loop operates in three steps: first, a decision or action is made based on a specific goal or objective; second, the decision's outcomes or results are observed and evaluated; finally, adjustments are made to refine future decisions or actions based on received feedback.

Consider a marketing team launching an advertising campaign to increase brand awareness and sales. They monitor the campaign's impact through metrics such as website traffic, social media engagement, and sales data. Depending on the campaign's success, they either continue with similar strategies or make adjustments like refining messaging or targeting different audiences. This iterative process allows for continuous enhancement of decision-making and optimization of marketing efforts.

Feedback loops offer several benefits, including learning from experiences and mistakes, enabling course correction and adaptation, promoting accountability and responsibility, and facilitating innovation and creativity. Individuals and organizations can optimize decision-making practices by actively engaging in this iterative cycle, leading to more effective and successful outcomes.

The Negative Feedback Loop

A prevalent challenge in decision-making is the negative feedback loop, a self-perpetuating pattern that can obstruct progress and result in subpar outcomes. This loop arises when a decision's consequences yield outcomes that amplify and sustain the original decision's negative aspects, generating a cycle of adverse effects. Grasping and identifying this feedback loop is vital for making informed choices and escaping its grip.

For example, consider a business owner who opts to cut costs by reducing their marketing budget. Initially, this choice may lead to immediate savings. However, as marketing efforts wane, the business's visibility and awareness suffer. With diminished visibility, customer acquisition and sales begin to decrease, leading to a drop in revenue and making it increasingly difficult to allocate adequate funds for future marketing. This situation reinforces the initial cost-cutting decision, trapping the business in a negative feedback loop with deteriorating performance.

Escaping the negative feedback loop necessitates proactive intervention and challenging assumptions. It involves acknowledging a decision's adverse effects and remaining open to strategy adjustments to mitigate those impacts. In the provided example, the business owner could break the cycle by reevaluating their marketing budget reduction decision and exploring alternative approaches. By investing in targeted marketing endeavors and closely monitoring results, they can reverse the decline and transition towards a positive trajectory.

Detecting negative feedback loops demands a thorough assessment of cause-and-effect relationships within a decision-making context. This process entails examining potential long-term consequences of choices and comprehending the interdependencies among various factors. Actively seeking feedback, monitoring outcomes, and adjusting strategies accordingly enables individuals and organizations to disrupt negative feedback loops and generate positive momentum toward their objectives.

Hence, the negative feedback loop presents a common decision-making challenge, where a decision's consequences perpetuate adverse outcomes, culminating in a self-reinforcing cycle. Identifying and proactively addressing this pattern is crucial for achieving desired outcomes and making informed choices. By understanding cause-and-effect relationships and adapting strategies as needed, individuals and organizations can surmount the negative feedback loop, paving the way for positive growth and success.

The Positive Feedback Loop

The positive feedback loop is a captivating phenomenon that significantly influences decision-making. It refers to a cycle where a minor change or action leads to an amplified effect, reinforcing the initial decision or behavior. This feedback loop creates a snowball effect, with outcomes growing more pronounced and impactful over time. Depending on the original decision or action, positive feedback loops can have both favorable and unfavorable consequences.

Consider an example of an entrepreneur who develops a new product and invests in targeted marketing efforts for a niche audience. As a result, they generate substantial interest and sales within that niche. The positive feedback loop emerges when initial sales and positive customer feedback increase brand visibility and reputation, attracting more customers, creating higher demand, and generating even more sales. The cycle continues, with each success reinforcing the initial decision to focus on that niche audience.

This scenario illustrates how a small decision, such as targeting a specific audience, can create a cascading effect amplifying desired outcomes, underscoring the importance of recognizing and harnessing positive feedback loops in decision-making.

However, acknowledge that positive feedback loops can also yield negative results. For example, if a business disregards customer feedback and neglects product flaws, negative word-of-mouth may spread quickly, causing sales to decline and damaging the company's reputation. The feedback loop exacerbates the initial problem, emphasizing promptly addressing issues to avoid harmful cycles.

Comprehending positive feedback loops enables decision-makers to recognize the potential for exponential growth or decline based on initial actions. Individuals and organizations can make decisions that produce long-lasting and compounding positive effects by proactively identifying opportunities to leverage positive feedback loops. This understanding accentuates the need for strategic and intentional decision-making, considering both immediate outcomes and the potential for positive feedback loops to drive sustained success.

Creating a Feedback Loop

Establishing a feedback loop is an invaluable technique in decision-making, promoting continuous improvement by enabling learning from decision outcomes and facilitating necessary adjustments. The foundation of an effective feedback loop involves deliberate, systematic feedback collection and analysis to inform future decisions.

Begin by **defining clear, measurable goals or desired outcomes**, which allow for the identification of specific metrics or indicators to evaluate decision success or effectiveness. Metrics may be quantitative, such as sales figures or customer satisfaction ratings, or qualitative, like stakeholder feedback or performance observations.

With metrics in place, consistently **gather feedback and data from various sources**, including customers, colleagues, experts, or self-reflection. Ensure feedback is specific, timely, and relevant to the decision, providing insights into the impact and consequences of choices.

Thoughtfully and objectively analyze collected feedback, identifying patterns, trends, and areas for improvement. **Consider feedback within the context of original goals and desired outcomes**, enabling the recognition of decision-making process strengths and weaknesses, areas requiring adjustments, and growth opportunities.

Implement changes that address identified improvement areas or capitalize on strengths based on analysis insights. Iteratively applying feedback and making adaptations enhances decision-making effectiveness over time.

A product development example demonstrates creating a feedback loop. Suppose a software developer aims to create an intuitive, user-friendly interface for a new application. They gather feedback from beta testers regarding usability and overall user experience. Analyzing the feedback reveals users struggling with a specific feature, prompting the developer to adjust the feature's design and functionality. An updated version is released to beta testers, who provide feedback indicating significant user experience improvements due to changes made.

By incorporating feedback into the decision-making process, the developer identifies improvement areas, makes necessary adjustments, and enhances the product's overall quality. This iterative feedback loop allows for continuous learning, adaptation, and improved outcomes based on real-world experiences.

Feedback Loops for Different Purposes

Feedback loops enhance our lives, from individual and team productivity to product development and personal improvement. The key is understanding the factors influencing changes in approaches and functions to increase efficiency. Inputs such as emails, customer inquiries, and to-do lists, and outputs like proposals, customer meetings, and blog posts can help refine productivity strategies.

In **product development**, feedback loops enable continuous improvement. Early iterations of products, such as typewriters, telephones, or firearms, underwent numerous changes and modifications based on user feedback, resulting in enhanced functionality.

Customer experience feedback loops also provide valuable insights for businesses. Sources may include restaurant comment cards, automated phone call recordings, or online feedback forms. Regardless of the medium, interpreting and using data to guide implementation decisions is crucial for optimizing customer experiences.

Lastly, **personal improvement feedback loops** contribute to individual growth. Although receiving criticism can be challenging, embracing feedback from friends, family, therapists, or self-reflection can lead to meaningful self-improvement steps. By implementing feedback loops across various domains, individuals and organizations can continually learn, adapt, and achieve success.

Improving Feedback Loops

Here are four suggested ways to make your feedback loops better:

- **Speed.** Real-time action should be the goal. The quicker you can implement the result of the feedback, the better impression you will create.

- **Measurability**. Have a metric by which to measure the value of feedback.

- **Context.** To improve feedback loops, one must consider the broader objective. However, understand the specific context in which feedback is given to ensure its effective application.

- **Motivation.** Caring about the feedback results is essential to improving and succeeding in creating positive outcomes.

Serving as a continuous improvement mechanism, a feedback loop systematically collects and employs feedback to shape future decisions. The chapter emphasized the importance of establishing clear goals, obtaining specific and pertinent feedback, and analyzing it to pinpoint improvement areas or leverage strengths. By implementing a feedback loop, individuals and organizations can benefit from iterative learning, resulting in refined decision-making and superior outcomes.

The chapter also examined the differences between positive and negative feedback loops, elucidating their impact on decision-making processes. Equipped with the knowledge to create an effective feedback loop, readers can utilize this powerful technique for ongoing learning, adaptation, and informed decision-making that fosters success.

Chapter 13:
Decision-Making Traps to Avoid

Making bad decisions is something we all experience at some point in our lives. While we do learn from these experiences, sometimes good decisions turn bad because of circumstances beyond our control. In those situations, taking control of what we can and mitigating the results is indispensable. To minimize bad decision-making, we must be aware of traps we should avoid falling into. This chapter aims to help us avoid these traps by explaining what they are and how they can be managed to create optimal decision-making conditions.

First Impressions

In the decision-making process, individuals often rely on initial impressions of available information, which can sometimes lead to traps that must be avoided. One such trap involves making hasty judgments based on limited data, potentially resulting in incomplete or inaccurate conclusions.

For example, considering an investment in a stock that has seen significant growth over recent months is a wise choice. However, further examination of the company's financial reports might reveal growing debt and potential losses, leading to a reevaluation of the investment.

Another pitfall is confirmation bias, where we seek evidence that supports our pre-existing opinions and dismiss contradictory information. Take the scenario of evaluating two job candidates; if you already hold a positive view of one and a negative view of the other, you may subconsciously focus on details that confirm your biases, possibly overlooking crucial factors and hiring the wrong candidate.

To sidestep these decision-making traps, it is crucial to recognize the limitations of first impressions and actively pursue additional information when making important decisions.

Maintaining the Status Quo

The status quo trap stems from fear of the unknown, risk aversion, and the appeal of stability. As a result, we may cling to familiar routines and approaches, stifling personal and professional growth.

To avoid the status quo trap, challenge your comfort zones and view change as an opportunity for growth. Cultivate a mindset of curiosity, openness, and adaptability, and ask thought-provoking questions about the potential benefits of stepping outside your comfort zone.

Additionally, gather diverse insights and seek different perspectives before making crucial decisions. Engage with trusted mentors or professionals in relevant fields for fresh viewpoints and new possibilities.

Ultimately, breaking free from the status quo requires courage and embracing change. Though it may feel uncomfortable initially, it can lead to personal and professional growth.

Consistency

While our brains are wired to seek coherence in thoughts, beliefs, and actions, inflexible adherence to consistency can hinder our ability to consider new information or adapt our approach.

This trap often manifests as an attachment to initial decisions or opinions, even when presented with evidence suggesting alternative options. The desire for coherence and avoidance of cognitive dissonance can blind us to new possibilities, preventing optimal decision-making.

For instance, the sunk cost fallacy demonstrates how consistency can lead to poor decisions. When heavily invested in a project, one may feel compelled to continue despite evidence that it is no longer viable. Additionally, relying on past experiences or familiar patterns can be problematic when they no longer apply to current situations.

To sidestep the consistency trap, cultivate a critical thinking mindset and open-mindedness. Recognize that consistency should serve as a means to achieve optimal outcomes rather than an inflexible rule. Be willing to challenge your beliefs, seek diverse perspectives, and remain open to change based on new information.

Ultimately, achieving consistency in decision-making involves rational analysis, consideration of various options, and adaptability to changing circumstances.

Expert Advice

While seemingly valuable for decision-making, expert advice can sometimes lead to limitations and biases. Solely relying on such guidance may narrow our perspective and hinder the exploration of alternative viewpoints or creative solutions. As such, recognize that experts have their own biases, limited experiences, and potential conflicts of interest. Uncritically accepting expert advice without evaluating its relevance to our unique situation can result in suboptimal decisions.

Take, for example, a business owner seeking advice on expanding their product line. Upon consulting an industry expert, they are advised to focus exclusively on high-end luxury products. However, the business owner neglects to consider factors such as target market, budget constraints, and competition. By following the expert's advice without question, they miss opportunities to cater to a broader customer base or explore untapped market segments.

Treat expert advice as just one component of the decision-making process to circumvent this trap. Incorporate additional information from data analysis, market research, and stakeholder insights. Utilize a comprehensive approach that combines expert opinions with personal knowledge, experience, and intuition. Synthesizing diverse perspectives and critically assessing expert advice within specific circumstances make more balanced and informed decisions.

The Sunk Cost Fallacy

The Sunk Cost Fallacy, a prevalent cognitive bias, can significantly influence decision-making. This fallacy arises when individuals make choices based on previous investments or sunk costs instead of evaluating the current situation objectively. The trap can keep us stuck in unproductive or disadvantageous circumstances as we feel obligated to continue investing time, money, or effort due to past commitments. However, succumbing to the Sunk Cost Fallacy obstructs progress and results in poor decision-making outcomes.

Our inherent aversion to loss contributes to the power of the Sunk Cost Fallacy. We often view sunk costs as losses and strive to avoid them. This fear clouds our judgment, preventing objective evaluation of potential benefits or risks associated with a decision. Instead, we fixate on recovering our initial investment, even when it no longer makes rational sense.

Emotional attachment can further reinforce the Sunk Cost Fallacy. We may form emotional connections to past investments, such as projects, relationships, or personal endeavors. This attachment hinders our ability to make rational decisions, as preserving our emotional investment becomes the priority over objectively assessing current circumstances and prospects.

To overcome the Sunk Cost Fallacy, adopt a mindset shift and embrace letting go of past investments. Acknowledge that past investments are irrecoverable and should not dictate future choices. Focus on present and future potential outcomes, using objective criteria like costs, benefits, and goal alignment for assessments.

An effective strategy to counter the Sunk Cost Fallacy is envisioning starting anew. By mentally detaching from past investments and evaluating decisions as if starting from scratch, we gain a fresh perspective and make more rational choices. Additionally, seeking input from others without emotional investment in the situation can offer valuable insights and help break the cycle of the Sunk Cost Fallacy.

The Psychology

Behavioral studies have revealed that there are five identifiable psychological factors that influence us in matters of the sunken cost effect.

Loss Aversion

The psychology of loss aversion exerts a powerful influence on our minds, often causing us to prioritize avoiding losses over pursuing potential gains. This phenomenon is evident in various situations, such as gambling, where the fear of losing money outweighs the desire to take risks and potentially make more money. The sunk cost fallacy contributes to this mindset by compelling us to stick with poor investment decisions due to our discomfort when facing losses.

Framing

Positive framing appeals to external information and our internal desire to project positivity. For instance, when deciding whether to continue or shut down a YouTube channel that falls short of expectations, the negative framing of shutting down encompasses the loss of invested money and the perception of failure. In contrast, positive framing encourages perseverance, creating an image of success in the eyes of others and ourselves.

Unfounded Optimism

Thorough due diligence is crucial when starting a business or making investments, yet we often overlook shortcomings or inconsistencies during this process. Optimism can cloud our judgment, leading us to believe we are less likely to experience negative outcomes than others. This unfounded or misplaced optimism significantly affects decision-making, particularly when embarking on new business ventures.

Personal Responsibility

It is generally easier to change a decision made by someone else that leads to unfavorable consequences than to alter a decision we made ourselves. When we have a personal stake in a decision, we develop an emotional attachment and a sense of responsibility. This attachment can make it challenging to objectively evaluate the decision's effectiveness and make necessary adjustments.

The Desire to Not Appear Wasteful

When we spend money on something, we naturally want to maximize its utility to feel that we have obtained our money's worth. However, this desire can drive us to persist with subpar options even when recognizing better alternatives. For example, persisting with inferior software for internal communication when a superior option is available contradicts rationality, as it is illogical to use a less effective solution to avoid wastefulness.

The Gambler's Fallacy

The Gambler's Fallacy is a cognitive bias often arising in decision-making, particularly when dealing with chance or probability. It stems from the mistaken belief that past events or outcomes will influence future ones, despite no logical or causal connection between them.

Consider a casino scenario where a gambler plays roulette, and the ball has landed on black for ten consecutive spins. The gambler assumes red is due soon, believing the universe must balance or correct the outcomes. However, each roulette spin is an independent event unaffected by previous results.

The Gambler's Fallacy can also manifest in other contexts, such as stock market investments. Investors might assume that a stock experiencing consecutive gains will soon decline, or vice versa. This notion disregards the factors influencing stock market performance and that past trends do not guarantee future outcomes.

This fallacy originates from our innate tendency to seek patterns and impose order on random events. Our minds crave predictability and control, leading us to assign significance to patterns or streaks that may be purely coincidental.

Recognizing and avoiding the Gambler's Fallacy is vital for making sound decisions. This requires a conscious effort to base decisions on relevant information, statistical probabilities, and logical reasoning rather than perceived patterns or false assumptions about future outcomes.

Mitigating the influence of the Gambler's Fallacy involves approaching decision-making with a clear understanding of probability and randomness. Adopting a rational mindset means acknowledging that each event is independent and past outcomes hold no sway over future ones.

By sidestepping the Gambler's Fallacy, we can make more informed choices, minimizing the risk of decisions based on flawed reasoning. Recognizing the fallacy enables us to rely on objective data, accurately analyze probabilities, and ultimately increase our chances of achieving desired outcomes.

The Hot-Hand Fallacy

The Hot-Hand Fallacy, an intriguing phenomenon in decision-making, challenges our intuitive grasp of streaks and patterns. This fallacy refers to the misconception that a series of successes boost the likelihood of future triumphs. Although widely believed, the Hot-Hand Fallacy indicates that such perceived streaks are statistical fluctuations and do not reliably forecast future outcomes.

When witnessing a basketball player scoring consecutive shots or a gambler winning several rounds consecutively, we naturally assume they have a *"hot hand"* and are more likely to keep winning. This fallacy arises from our innate tendency to discern patterns and assign meaning to random occurrences. However, statistical studies consistently demonstrate that individual performance in most fields, including sports, gambling, and even investing, is largely independent of prior results.

The Hot-Hand Fallacy can be understood by examining randomness and probability laws. In a truly random process, each event is independent and unaffected by previous instances, meaning a successful outcome on one occasion does not increase the odds of success on the next. Recognizing that perceived streaks often result from random fluctuations within underlying probabilities rather than inherent skill or momentum is crucial.

Grasping the Hot-Hand Fallacy has significant implications for decision-making across various life aspects. In sports, coaches and players may make decisions based on the hot hand illusion, leading to suboptimal strategies and misguided expectations. Likewise, investors might assume that a winning streak in the stock market will persist indefinitely, potentially resulting in poor investment choices and financial losses.

To evade the pitfalls of the Hot-Hand Fallacy, base decisions on objective data, statistical analysis, and a clear understanding of probability. Acknowledging that past successes do not guarantee future outcomes allows for more rational and informed choices. Adopting an evidence-based mindset and thorough analysis enables us to traverse decision-making with greater clarity, steering clear of illusory streaks and making choices rooted in sound reasoning.

Various decision-making pitfalls can impede our ability to make well-informed choices. As such, the impact of first impressions, the temptation to adhere to the status quo, the significance of consistency, and the risks associated with relying exclusively on expert advice. Furthermore, we investigated three fallacies that frequently obscure our judgment: the sunk cost fallacy, the gambler's fallacy, and the hot hand fallacy. Recognizing and being conscious of these traps enhances our decision-making skills, sidestepping irrational and misguided choices. By liberating ourselves from the constraints of these pitfalls, we are better equipped to make more informed, objective, and effective decisions across all aspects of our lives

Conclusion

Decision-making, a skill applicable to various areas of life, plays a vital role in navigating complex situations and achieving desired outcomes. **Chapter 1** provided an in-depth exploration of decision-making's core elements, including choice, information, and preference. By understanding the interconnection between these components, we established a strong foundation for effective decision-making across business, healthcare, education, and personal life.

Building upon this foundation, **Chapter 2** emphasized the importance of asking critical WH questions when making decisions. We examined the significance of identifying the decision, understanding motivations, defining goals, recognizing contributing factors, and assessing existing knowledge. Additionally, we recognized the value of considering the people involved, the timing, and the location of the issue. By addressing these questions comprehensively, we laid the groundwork for informed decision-making.

Chapter 3 highlighted the crucial step of documenting the problem in decision-making. We explored practical techniques for adequate documentation, focusing on clear and concise writing, in-depth descriptions, and relevant details. Mastering the art of documentation gave us a comprehensive understanding of the problem, facilitating thoughtful analysis and decision-making.

As the backbone of informed decision-making, data took center stage in **Chapter 4.** We delved into various data types, including qualitative and quantitative, and emphasized the importance of utilizing both. Assessing internal and external data sources while avoiding common pitfalls during data collection became an essential skill. By mastering the art of gathering relevant data, we gained valuable insights for making well-informed decisions.

Meanwhile, **Chapter 5** addressed the significant impact of cognitive biases on decision-making. We examined the concept of cognitive bias, its causes, signs, and its influence on choices. Various biases, such as confirmation bias, anchoring effect, and groupthink, were explored, along with strategies to overcome them. By identifying and addressing cognitive biases, we aimed for more objective decision-making.

Exploring alternatives became the focus of **Chapter 6**, recognizing its importance in decision-making. We examined techniques for generating creative alternatives and considering previous and disregarded solutions. By expanding our perspectives and exploring various options, we aimed to make more robust and innovative decisions.

Subsequently, **Chapter 7** emphasized the necessity of viewing decisions from different angles. We explored tools like brainstorming, conversations with others, wish lists, and creative methods to facilitate diverse perspectives. Assessing associated costs, risks, trade-offs, benefits, and the probability of success became integral to the decision-making process. By embracing diverse viewpoints and avoiding common pitfalls, we enhanced the overall quality of our decision-making.

Values and goals took center stage in **Chapter 8**, shaping our decision-making journey. We focused on defining our values and goals and understanding how they influenced our choices. Aligning alternatives with our core principles and considering the ideal situation became crucial. By grounding our decisions in our values and goals, we ensured choices that resonated with our authentic selves.

Then, **Chapter 9** delved into the integral role of risk analysis in decision-making. We explored the steps involved, including risk identification, estimation, perception, and evaluation. By gaining a thorough understanding of the risks associated with our decisions, we were able to mitigate potential pitfalls and make informed choices.

Building upon that, **Chapter 10** focused on the concept of an action plan and its significance in translating decisions into tangible results. We examined creating a detailed list of actions, setting SMART goals, acquiring necessary resources, establishing timelines, and monitoring progress. Through the development of a structured action plan, we could effectively implement our decisions and achieve the desired outcomes.

Recognizing the challenges inherent in decision implementation, **Chapter 11** offered strategies to address risks during this crucial phase. We explored methods such as monitoring actions, employing preventative or acceleration measures, and implementing conditional actions. By proactively managing risks, we increased the likelihood of successful implementation.

Shifting our focus to the importance of feedback, **Chapter 12** explored the role of feedback loops in decision-making. We uncovered various forms of feedback loops and discussed how they contribute to enhancing decision-making processes. Additionally, we examined different feedback loops tailored to specific purposes and strategies for improving their effectiveness.

Lastly, in **Chapter 13**, we focused on the potential traps that could hinder optimal decision-making. We examined common pitfalls, including first impressions, maintaining the status quo, consistency bias, reliance on expert advice, the sunk cost fallacy, and unfounded optimism. By developing an understanding of these traps, we were equipped to navigate them and make decisions based on sound reasoning, avoiding fallacies.

Through the exploration of these chapters, we cultivated a comprehensive understanding of decision-making. Armed with the knowledge and tools acquired, we were empowered to make effective choices in various aspects of life.

Glossary

Action plan. Detailed strategy for decision implementation.

Alternatives. Different options available for decision-making.

Assessment. Evaluation or judgment.

Assumptions. Beliefs taken for granted without proof.

Audio recordings. Capturing and documenting spoken information and discussions.

Benchmarking. Comparing the current problem or situation with similar cases or **standards.**

Benefits. Positive outcomes of a decision.

Bias. Prejudice towards a choice without rational justification.

Choice. Selecting one option from a set of alternatives, considering outcomes and consequences.

Clear goals. Well-defined objectives and desired outcomes.

Consequences. Results following a decision.

Cost-benefit analysis. Assessing costs and benefits of alternatives.

Credibility. Believability or trustworthiness.

Criteria. Standards used to assess decisions.

Critical thinking. Objectively analyzing alternatives and making well-reasoned decisions.

Cultural context. Beliefs influencing decision-making.

Data visualization. Presenting information visually.

Decision types. Categories of decisions, including strategic, tactical, and operational.

Decision-making processes. The series of steps and actions taken to make choices and reach a conclusion.

Decision-making skills. Ability necessary for effective decisions.

Decision-making. The process of evaluating and analyzing alternatives to choose an option.

Deconstruction. Breaking down a problem or issue into smaller components for analysis.

Demographic factors. Characteristics impacting decisions.

Documentation. Recording and preserving information related to a decision-making process or problem.

Emotional impact. Effect of a problem or decision on emotional well-being.

Empirical. Based on observation or experience.

Environmental factors. External elements influencing decisions.

Ethical considerations. Moral principles guiding decision-making.

Execution. Implementing a decision.

Factual. Based on facts or reality.

Feedback loop. Continuous cycle where choices and preferences shape decision-making.

Goals. Desired objectives to be achieved through a decision.

Historical context. Past events shaping decisions.

Holistic. Considering all relevant factors comprehensively.

Implementation. Putting a decision or plan into action.

In-depth analysis. Thorough examination and evaluation of a problem or situation.

Information. Relevant data, facts, or knowledge that aids decision-making.

Insights. Deep understanding or perceptions.

Introspection. Examining one's thoughts, emotions, and actions for self-reflection and analysis.

Intuition. Ability to understand or know something instinctively.

Intuitive. Based on instinct or gut feelings.

Memory errors. Inaccuracies or distortions in human memory.

Objectivity. Unbiased and impartial.

Operational decisions. Lower-level choices impacting day-to-day functioning.

Opportunity cost. Potential benefits or opportunities forgone when choosing one option over another.

Outcomes. Results of a decision.

Patterns and trends. Recurring themes or characteristics in decision-making that provide insights.

Personal growth. Self-improvement through decision-making.

Perspectives. Different viewpoints on a decision.

Pitfalls. Hidden problems or difficulties.

Precision. Accuracy, clarity, and exactness in analyzing and describing.

Preference. Individual emotions, values, and priorities influencing choices.

Problem documentation. Recording and capturing information related to a problem or issue.

Professional development. Continuous improvement and growth of skills in a specific field.

Qualitative. Data that describes qualities or characteristics.

Quantitative data. Numerical information and statistics.

Rationale. Reasoning or justification behind a decision.

Reference point. Basis for evaluating or understanding future situations or decisions.

Reflection. Thoughtful consideration and analysis of past experiences and decisions.

Reliable. Dependable and trustworthy.

Research. Systematic investigation and study to gather information and acquire knowledge.

Resource allocation. Distributing and utilizing resources effectively in decisions.

Resource optimization. Maximizing resource utilization for optimal outcomes.

Risk management. Identifying, assessing, and mitigating decision risks.

Risks. Potential negative outcomes of a decision.

Sifting. Sorting or filtering through to extract what is valuable or relevant.

Solutions. Resolutions for problems.

Speculation. Forming opinions or theories without definite evidence.

Stakeholders. Individuals or groups affected by a decision.

Statistical modeling. Analyzing data mathematically for decision insights.

Strategic decisions. High-level choices shaping long-term organization direction.

Strategy. Well-thought-out plan for a goal.

Tactical decisions. Intermediate-level choices influencing immediate operations.

Templates. Pre-designed structures or formats for organizing and documenting information.

Thought process. Cognitive steps and reasoning involved in making decisions.

Trade-off. Exchanging one thing for another when deciding, considering benefits and drawbacks.

Validity. Logical or factual soundness.

Video footage. Recording and preserving visual content related to decision-making.

Visual aids. Graphical tools used to visually represent and communicate information.

Well-being. Optimal physical, mental, and emotional health influenced by decisions.

Written notes. Recorded annotations capturing important information related to decision-making.

References

Brooker, K. (2018). *I was devastated:* Tim Berners-Lee, the man who created the world wide web, has some regrets. https://www.vanityfair.com/news/2018/07/the-man-who-created-the-world-wide-web-has-some-regrets

Cuesta.edu. (n.d.). *Decision-making and problem-solving.* https://www.cuesta.edu/student/resources/ssc/study_guides/critical_thinking/106_think_decisions.html

The Decision Lab. (n.d.). *Why do we think a random event is more or less likely to occur if it happened several times in the past?* https://thedecisionlab.com/biases/gamblers-fallacy

Decisioneducation.org. (n.d.). *Creative Alternatives:* There is Usually a Better Way. https://www.decisioneducation.org/decision-chain/creative-alternatives#:~:text=An%20alternative%20is%20one%20of,%2C%20and%20(4)%20doable

Decisionmakingconfidence.com (n.d.) *Common but invisible decision making traps.* https://www.decision-making-confidence.com/decision-making-traps.html

Decisionmakingsolutions.com. (n.d.). *Decision implementation* - Get the desired resultsd during the manage step. https://www.decision-making-solutions.com/decision-implementation.html

Forsey, C. (2018, July 6). *The definition of negative and positive feedback loops in 200 words or less.* https://blog.hubspot.com/marketing/feedback-loop

Get2growth.com. (n.d.). *The power of feedback loops.* https://get2growth.com/feedback-loops/

Howe. (2021). Stanford Encyclopedia of Philosophy: Margaret Fuller. Https://Plato.Stanford.Edu/Entries/Fuller-Margaret/

MacNeil, C. (2022). *How the sunk cost fallacy influences our decisions.* https://asana.com/resources/sunk-cost-fallacy

Millar, E. (2017). *Dr. W. Edwards Deming:* Hero of quality. https://www.qad.com/blog/2017/10/dr-w-edwards-deming-hero-quality

Nasman, P. (2005). *Risk analysis* - A tool in decision making. https://www.diva-portal.org/smash/get/diva2:14614/FULLTEXT01.pdf

1000minds.com. (n.d.). 70 *inspirational decision-making quotes.* https://www.1000minds.com/decision-making/decision-quotes

Online.usi. (2021). *Risk assessment when making business decisions.* https://online.usi.edu/degrees/business/mba/general/risk-assessment-when- -decisions/

Sagepub.com. *Carol Grbich:* The Flinders University of South Australia. https://us.sagepub.com/en-us/nam/author/carol-grbich

Sailus, C. (n.d.). *John Wooden's pyramid of success.* https://study.com/academy/lesson/john-woodens-pyramid-of-success.html

Shockley, J. (2020). *A creepy ghost town in Kentucky, Paradise is the stuff nightmares are made of.* https://www.onlyinyourstate.com/kentucky/ghost-town-ky/

Simmons, R. (2022). *4 pitfalls to avoid in data driven decision making.* https://www.novelleonline.com/post/4-pitfalls-to-avoid-in-data-driven-decision-making

Socialsciencespace.com. (2023). *David Dunning on the Dunning-Kruger Effect.* https://www.socialsciencespace.com/2023/01/david-dunning-on-the-dunning-kruger-effect/

Studentlesson.com. (2022). *Understanding an action plan, its importance, and how to write it.* https://studentlesson.com/understanding-action-plan-it-importance-and-how-to-write-it/#:~:text=An%20action%20plan%20is%20an,the%20process%20of%20strategic%20planning

Weprin, A. (2022). *Nate Silver out at ABC News as Disney layoffs once again hit news division.* https://www.hollywoodreporter.com/business/digital/nate-silver-leaves-538-abc-news-disney-layoffs-1235401689/

Printed in Great Britain
by Amazon

52104179R00099